THE LIFE OF FAITH

THE LIFE OF FAITH

ARTHUR W PINK

CHRISTIAN FOCUS PUBLICATIONS

© 1993 Christian Focus Publications Ltd
ISBN 1 85792 047 3

Published by
Christian Focus Publications Ltd
Geanies House, Fearn, Ross-shire,
IV20 1TW, Scotland, Great Britain.

Cover design
by
Donna Macleod

Contents

Milestones in the life of Arthur W Pink

1886: Born in Nottingham, England.

1908: Converted.

1910: Pink crossed the Atlantic, intending to study for two years at the Moody Bible Institute in Chicago. However, after two months he decided to take a pastoral charge in Colorado. Further charges followed in California, Kentucky and South Carolina.

1916: Married Vera Russell.

1921: Pink decided to cease pastoral ministry and instead concentrate on writing and Bible conference work. In addition to several books, Pink commenced in 1922 a monthly magazine entitled *Studies in the Scriptures*, which he continued to edit and publish until his death. It is from this magazine that most of the material currently available in books today is taken.

1925: Moved to Australia where they remained until 1928. After a short stay in England they went back to the USA for several years before finally returning to Britain in 1934. Despite preaching for various denominations, Pink was not able to secure a permanent preaching position.

1936 to 1952: he concentrated on producing *Studies in the Scriptures*, first in Hove, England and then in Stornoway in the Outer Hebrides of Scotland.

1952: Died in Stornoway, Scotland.

Introduction

The best of Arthur W Pink's writings are those in which he explains the practical aspects of the Christian life. He was aware that the interest of many professing Christians during the period in which he lived focused on doctrinal matters, in particular, unfulfilled prophecy. In addition he regarded much of the practical teaching that was given as shallow and not coming up to scriptural demands. To combat this he emphasised in his magazine, *Studies in the Scriptures*, the fact that believers are to live according to the Scriptures as well as believe the truth taught in them.

There are several books by Pink available today, of which perhaps his best known work is *The Sovereignty of God*. Most of them are articles taken from his magazine. He wrote on a wide variety of topics including the attributes of God, the person and work of Christ, the Holy Spirit, communion with God, spiritual growth and biblical characters. Some other articles from *Studies in the Scriptures* have never been reprinted.

This publication entitled *The Life of Faith* is a selection drawn from published books and magazine articles. The intention is to stress Pink's main emphases, beginning with what God has done for his people and then focusing on certain aspects of the Christian life.

Chapter 1 shows the design of God in purposing the death of Christ on behalf of his people. Chapter 2 unfolds the work of the Spirit in the Christian Dispensation; while chapter 3, clearly states the nature of Christian assurance.

The remaining chapters concentrate on different aspects of

the Christian life. Chapter 4 stresses the need for spiritual development, and Pink makes interesting observations on the meaning of progressive sanctification. In Chapter 5, Pink brings together two important individual spiritual disciplines, Bible reading and prayer. Chapter 6 outlines the believer's relationship to God's moral law, summarised in the Ten Commandments.

In Chapter 7 Pink examines a common feature of Christian experience - backsliding and restoration as seen in the life of David. Chapter 8 also looks at an individual, Elisha, to see the way believers, and in particular, ministers can be tested by God. Christian submission is the theme of chapter 9 - an attitude to be worked out in all relationships of life. The final selection, Grace Preparing For Glory, is an exhortation to live appropriately in the light of the Second Coming of Jesus.

The overall theme is one of providing a balanced approach to living in a Christian way.

A small amount of editing has been done but each selection is essentially as Pink originally wrote it.

Original source of selected chapters:
Chapter 1: *The Satisfaction of Christ* (1930-31)
Chapters 2,3: *The Holy Spirit* (1933-37)
Chapter 4: *Spiritual Growth* (1944-46)
Chapter 5: *Profiting from the Word* (1930-32)
Chapter 6: *Gleanings in Exodus* (1924-29)
Chapter 7: *The Life of David* (1932-39)
Chapter 8: *The Life of Elisha* (1943-45)
Chapter 9: *Studies in the Scriptures* 1946
Chapter 10: *Studies in the Scriptures* 1936

CHAPTER 1

The Design of the Atonement

What was the purpose of the Eternal Three in sending Christ Jesus into this world? What was the incarnation of the Son of God intended to accomplish? What were his sufferings and obedience ordained to effect? Concerning this all-important matter the most erroneous ideas have been entertained, ideas at direct variance with Holy Scripture, ideas most dishonouring to God. Even where these awful errors have not been fully espoused, sufficient of their evil leaven has been received to corrupt the pure truth which many good men have held. In other instances, where this great subject has been largely neglected, only the vaguest and haziest conceptions are entertained. Sad it is to see what small place this vital theme now has in most pulpits, and in the thoughts and studies of the majority of professing Christians.

'Known unto God are all his works from the beginning of the world' (Acts 15:18). Everything God does is according to design: all is the working out of 'the eternal purpose which he purposed in Christ Jesus our Lord' (Ephesians 3:11). God had a design in creation (Revelation 4:10). He has a design in providence (Romans 8:28). And he has a design or purpose in the Satisfaction which was wrought by Christ (1 Peter 1:20). What, then, was that purpose? This is not a speculative question, but one of the utmost moment. Surely the right answer to it must be the one which upholds the glory of God.

9

Therefore any answer which carries with it the inevitable corollaries of a dishonoured Father, a disgraced Saviour and a defeated Holy Spirit, *cannot* be the right one. Redemption is the glory of all God's works, but it would be an everlasting disgrace of them if it should fail to effect whatsoever it was ordained to accomplish.

One conception, now widely held, is that Christ came here to remove certain barriers which stood in the way of God's grace flowing forth to fallen creatures. This theory is that Christ's death took away that hindrance which the Divine justice interposed to mercy being extended to transgressors of the law. Holders of this view suppose the great Atonement was merely the procuring unto God a right for his pardoning of sin. The words of Arminius are: 'God had a mind and will to do good to humankind, but could not by reason of sin, his justice being in the way; whereupon he sent Christ to remove that obstacle, so that he might, upon the prescribing of what condition he pleased, and its being by them fulfilled, have mercy on them.' Sad it is to find so many today echoing the errors of this misguided man.

The error in the above theory is easily exposed. If it were true that the design of Christ's satisfaction was to acquire a right unto his Father, that notwithstanding his justice he might save sinners, then did he rather die to redeem a liberty *unto* God, than a liberty *from evil* unto his people; that a door might be opened for God to come out in mercy to us, rather than that a way should be opened for us to go in unto him. This is certainly a turning of things upside down. And where, we may ask, is there a word in Scripture to support such a grotesque idea? Does Scripture declare that God sent his Son out of love to himself or out of love unto us? Does Scripture affirm that

Christ died to procure something for God, or for his people? Does Scripture teach that the obstacles were thrown out by Divine justice or that our sins were what Christ came here to remove? There can be only one answer to these questions.

Again: this theory would reduce the whole work of Christ to a costly experiment which might or might not succeed, inasmuch as according to this conception, there is still some condition which the sinner himself must fulfil ere he can be benefited by that mercy which God would bestow upon him. But *that* is a flat denial of the fatal effects of the Fall, a repudiation of the total depravity of man. Those who are spiritually dead in sins are quite *incapable* of performing any spiritual conditions. As well offer to a man who is stone blind a thousand dollars on condition that he sees, as offer something spiritual to one who has *no* capacity to discern it: see John 3:3, 1 Corinthians 2:14. Such a view as this is as far removed from the truth as is light from darkness. Such a view, reduced to plain terms, comes to this: if the sinner believes, then Christ died for him; if the sinner does not believe, then Christ did not die for him; thus the sinner's act is made the cause of its own object, as though his believing would make that *to be* which otherwise was not. To such insane absurdities are the opposers of grace driven.

How different the plain teaching of the Word! Christ came here to fulfil his agreement in the Everlasting Covenant. In that covenant a certain work was prescribed. Upon his performance of it a certain reward was promised. That work was that Christ should make a perfect satisfaction unto God on behalf of each and all of his people. That reward was that all the blessings procured and purchased by him should be infallibly bestowed on each and all of his people.

> God out of his infinite love to his elect, sent his dear Son in the
> fullness of time, whom he had promised in the beginning of the
> world; to pay a ransom of infinite value and dignity, for the
> purchasing of eternal redemption, and bringing unto himself all and
> every one of those whom he had before ordained to eternal life, for
> the praise of his own glory. So that freedom from all the evil from
> which we are delivered, and an enjoyment of all the good things that
> are bestowed on us, in our traduction from death to life, from hell and
> wrath to heaven and glory, are the proper issues and effects of the
> death of Christ, as the meritorious cause of them all (John Owen).

We are now ready to answer our opening question. The
design of Christ's Satisfaction was

1. That God Might be Magnified.

'The LORD hath made all things for himself' (Proverbs 16:4).
The great end which God has in all his works is the promotion
of his own declarative glory: 'For of him, and through him,
and *to him*, are all things: to whom be glory for ever. Amen'
(Romans 11:36). It must be so. There is nothing outside
himself which can possibly supply any motive for him to act.
To assert the contrary would be to deny his self-sufficiency.
The aim of God in creation, in providence, and in redemption,
is the magnifying *of himself*. Everything else is subordinate to
this paramount consideration. We press this, because we are
living in an age of infidelity and practical atheism.

God predestinated his people unto 'the glory of his grace'
(Ephesians 1:6). Christ has 'received us to the glory of God'
(Romans 15:7). All the Divine promises for us are in Christ
'Amen, to the glory of God' (2 Corinthians 1:20). The
inheritance which we have obtained in Christ is in order that
'we should be to the praise of his glory' (Ephesians 1:12). The
Holy Spirit is given us as the earnest of our inheritance 'unto

the praise of his glory' (Ephesians 1:14). The very rejoicing of the believer is 'in hope of the glory of God' (Romans 5:2). Our thanksgiving is that it may 'redound to the glory of God' (2 Corinthians 4:15). This is the one design of all the benefits which we obtain from the Satisfaction of Christ, for 'we are filled with the fruits of righteousness which are by Jesus Christ unto the glory and praise of God' (Philippians 1:11). While very tongue shall yet 'confess that Jesus Christ is Lord to the glory of God the Father' (Philippians 2:11).

God had both a subservient and a supreme design in sending Christ into this world: the supreme design was to display his own glory, the subservient design was to save his elect unto his own glory. The former was accomplished by the manifestation of his blessed attributes, which is the chief design in all his works, pre-eminently so in his greatest and grandest work of all. The remainder of the chapter might well be devoted to the extension of this one thought. Through Christ's obedience and death God magnified his *law* (Isaiah 42:21). The law of God was more honoured by the Son's subjection to it, than it was dishonoured by the disobedience of all of Adam's race. God magnified his *love* by sending forth the Darling of his bosom to redeem worthless worms of the earth. He magnified his *justice*, for when sin (by imputation) was found upon his Son, he called for the sword to smite him (Zechariah 13:7). He magnified his *holiness*: his hatred of sin was more clearly shown at the Cross than it will be in the lake of fire. He magnified his *power* by sustaining the Mediator under such a load as was laid upon him. He magnified his *truth* by fulfilling his covenant engagements and bringing forth from the dead the great Shepherd of the sheep (Hebrews 13:20). He magnified his *grace* by imputing to the ungodly all

the merits of Christ. This, then, was the prime purpose of God
in the Atonement: to magnify himself.

2. That The God-Man Might be Glorified.

Christ is the Centre of all the counsels of the Godhead. He is
both the Alpha and Omega of their designs. All God's
thoughts concerning everything in heaven and in earth begin
and end in Christ. 'God created all things by Jesus Christ'
(Ephesians 3:9), and all things were created 'for him' (Colossians 1:16). As Mediator he is the only medium of union and
communion between God and the creature. 'That in the
dispensation of the fullness of times he might gather together
in one all things *in Christ*, both which are in heaven, and which
are on earth; in him' (Ephesians 1:10). Christ is the one
universal head in which God has summed up all things.
Therefore was the stupendous work of redemption given to
him that he might reconcile all things in heaven and earth unto
himself, and this, that a revenue of glory might come to him.

The man Christ Jesus was taken up into union with the
essential and eternal Word, God the Son, so that he might be
Jehovah's 'Fellow' (Zechariah 13:7). The man Christ Jesus was
predestinated unto the ineffable honour of union with the second
person in the Trinity. As such he is the head of the whole election
of grace, called by the Father, 'Mine elect, in whom my soul
delighteth' (Isaiah 42:1). As the God-man, the Father covenanted with him, appointed him as Surety, and assigned him
his work. As God-man, he had a covenant subsistence before
he became incarnate. This is clear from John 6:62: 'What and
if ye shall see the Son of *man* ascend up where he was *before*?'
It was as the God-man the Father 'sent' forth Christ on his
errand of mercy, and that for his personal glory.

As Judas went out to betray him, Christ said, 'Now is the Son of man glorified' (John 13:31). Within a few hours his stupendous undertaking would be accomplished. The Mediator was honoured, supremely honoured, by God's having committed to his care the mightiest work of all, a work which none other was capable of performing. To him was entrusted the task of glorifying God here on earth; of vanquishing his arch-enemy, the Devil; of redeeming his elect. To this he makes reference in John 17:4, 'I have glorified thee on the earth; I have finished the work which thou gavest me to do.' He had completed God's vast design, executed his decrees, fulfilled all his will.

Having so gloriously glorified the Father, the Father has proportionately glorified the Mediator. He has been exalted high above 'all principality and power, and might and dominion, and every name that is named, not only in this world, but also in that which is to come' (Ephesians 1:21). He has been elevated to 'the right hand of the Majesty on high' (Hebrews 1:3). He has been given all authority in heaven and in earth (Matthew 28:18). He has been given 'power over all flesh, that he should give eternal life to as many as the Father hast given him' (John 17:2). He has been given a name which is above every name, before which name every knee shall yet bow (Philippians 2:11). Speaking of Christ's finished work and the Father's rewarding thereof, the Psalmist said, 'His glory is great in thy salvation: honour and majesty hast thou laid upon him. For thou hast made him most blessed forever: thou hast made him exceeding glad with thy countenance' (Psalm 21:5, 6). This was the grand design of the Trinity: that the God-man should thus be glorified.

3. That God's Elect Might be Saved.

'For the Son of man is come to seek and to *save* that which was lost' (Luke 19:10). How different is this plain, positive and unqualified statement from the tale which nearly all preachers tell today! The story of the vast majority is that Christ came here to make salvation *possible* for sinners: he has done his part, now they must do theirs. To reduce the wondrous, finished, and glorious work of Christ to a merely making salvation possible is most dishonouring and insulting to him.

Christ came here to carry into effect God's sovereign purpose of election, to save a people already 'his' (Matthew 1:21) by covenant settlement. There are a people whom God hath 'from the beginning chosen unto salvation' (2 Thessalonians 2:13), and redemption was in order to the *accomplishing* of that decree. And if we believe what Scripture declares concerning the person of Christ, then we have indubitable proof that there can be no possible failure in connection with *his* mission. The Son of man, the Child born, was none other than 'the mighty God' (Isaiah 9:6). Therefore is he omniscient, and knows where to look for each of his lost ones; he is also omnipotent, and so cannot fail to deliver when they are found.

Observe that Luke 19:10 does not say that Christ came here to seek and to save *all* the lost. Of course it does not. Two thirds of human history had already run its course before Jesus was born. Half the human race was already in hell when he entered Bethlehem's manger. It was '*the* lost' (see Greek) for which he became incarnate. That is the awful condition in which God's elect are by nature. Lost! They have lost all knowledge of the true God, all liking for him, all desires after him. They have lost his image in which they were originally created, and have contracted the image of Satan. They have lost all knowledge of their own actual condition, for their understanding is darkened (Ephesians 4:18), they are spiritually dead in trespasses and sins (Ephesians 2:1). Totally unconscious of their terrible state they neither seek Christ nor realise their need of him.

Christ did not come here to see if there were any who would seek after him. Of course not. Romans 3:11 emphatically declares 'there is *none* that seeketh after God'. *Christ* is the seeker. Beautifully is that brought out by him in his parable of the lost sheep. A strayed dog or a lost horse will usually find its way back home. Not so a sheep: the longer it is free, the farther it strays from the fold. Hence, if that sheep is ever to be recovered, one must go after it. This is what Christ did, and which by his Spirit he is still doing. As Luke 15:4 declares, he goes 'after that which is lost until he *find* it'. But more: Christ came here not only to seek and find, but also to *save*. His words are, 'For the Son of man is come to seek and to *save* that which was lost.' Note it is not merely that he offers to, nor helps to, but that he actually *saves*. Such was the emphatic and unqualified declaration of the angel to Joseph, 'Thou shalt call his name Jesus, for he *shall save* his people from their sins' - not try to, not half do so, but actually *save* them.

Christ came here with a definitely defined object in view, and being who he is there is no possible room for any failure in his mission. Hence, before he came here, God declared that he should 'see of the travail of his soul and *be satisfied*' (Isaiah 53:10). As the Mediator he solemnly covenanted with the Father *to* save his people from their sins. He actually *purchased* them with his blood (Acts 20:28). He has wrought out for them a perfect salvation, therefore is he 'mighty to save'

(Isaiah 63:1). Blessedly is this illustrated in the immediate context of Luke 19:10. To Zacchaeus he said, 'Make haste, and come down; for today I *must* abide at thy house... This day is salvation come to this house, forasmuch as he also is a son of Abraham' (vv 5,9). Yes, 'a son of Abraham', one of the elect seed. Therefore we boldly say to the reader, If you belong to the sheep of Christ, you *must* be saved, even though now you may be quite unconscious of your lost condition. Though, like Saul of Tarsus, you may yet 'kick against the pricks', invincible grace *shall* conquer you, for it is written, 'Thy people shall be willing in the day of thy power' (Psalm 110:3).

'I am come *that* they might have life, and that they might have it more abundantly. I am the good Shepherd: the good Shepherd giveth his life for the sheep' (John 10:10,11). Here again we have clearly defined the *design* of Christ's mission and satisfaction. His sheep once possessed 'life', possessed it in their natural head, Adam. But when he fell, they fell; when he died, they died. As it is written, 'In Adam all die' (1 Corinthians 15:22). But by Christ, through his work, and in him their spiritual head, they obtain not only 'life', but 'more abundant' life; that is, a 'life' which as far excels what they lost in their first father, as the last Adam excels in his Person, the first Adam. Therefore it is written, 'The first Adam was made a living soul; the last Adam a quickening spirit' (1 Corinthians 15:45).

'As the Father hath life in himself, so hath he given to the Son to have life in himself' (John 6:26), which speaks of Christ as the God-man, the Mediator, as is clear from the words 'given to'. But that 'life' had to be 'laid down' (John 10:17) and received again in resurrection before it could be, efficaciously, bestowed on his people (John 12:24). It was as the Risen One that Christ was made 'a quickening spirit'. The first Adam was 'made a living soul' that he might communicate natural life to his posterity; the last Adam was 'made a quickening spirit' that he might impart spiritual life to all his seed. As the soul dwelling in Adam's body animated it and so made him to be a 'living soul', so the man Christ Jesus being united to the second Person of the Trinity, has constituted him a 'quickening spirit', i.e. quickening his mystical body, both now and hereafter. The life of the head is the life of his members.

The Christian first has a federal life *in* Christ before he has a vital life *from* Christ. Being legally one with Christ, this must be so. When Christ died his people died, when Christ was quickened his people were quickened 'together with' him (Ephesians 2:5). It is to this union with the life of Christ that Romans 5:17 refers: 'For if by one man's offence death reigned by one; much more they which receive abundance of grace and of the gift of righteousness shall reign in life by one, Jesus Christ.' Yes, there is a 'much more': the abundance of grace is greater than the demerits of sin, and the gift of righteousness exceeds that which was lost in Adam. The righteousness of God's elect far surpasses that which they possessed in innocence by the first Adam, for it is the righteousness of Christ, who is God. To this, neither the righteousness of Adam nor of angels can be compared. Those redeemed by Christ are not only recovered from the fall, but they are made to '*reign* in life' to which they had no title in their first parent. Since Christ is King, his people are made 'kings' too (Revelation 1:6).

The same aspect of truth is brought before us again in 2

Corinthians 5:14, 15: 'For the love of Christ constraineth us: because we thus judge *that* if one for all died, then all died. And for all he died, *that* they who live no longer to themselves should live, but to him who for them died and was raised again' (Bagster's Interlinear). Many have supposed that the last clause of verse 14 refers to those who are 'dead in sins', but *that* was true apart from the death of Christ! Nor does the spiritual death of Adam's fallen descendants render them capable of 'living unto' Christ, but the very reverse. No, it is, 'If one for all died' (i.e. for all his people), then they all died *in him*. Then in verse 15 we have stated the consequence and fruit of this: as the result of his rising from the dead, they 'live'. His act was, representatively, their act. The atoning death of Christ, on the ground of federal union and substitution, was also our death; see Galatians 2:20. So too his resurrection was, representatively, our resurrection: see Colossians 3:1. Thus, in Christ, God's elect have a 'more abundant' life than they ever had in unfallen Adam.

The same truth is set before us in 1 Peter 2:24, 'Who his own self bare our sins in his body on the tree, *that we*, being dead to sins, should live unto righteousness.' The second half of it expresses the Divine design in appointing Christ to be federally and vicariously the Bearer of his peoples' sins. Christ's death was their death: they are 'dead to sins', not to 'sinning'! Let the reader compare Romans 6:2 and the apostle's exposition in the next nine verses. Further, Christ's resurrection was their resurrection: they 'live', legally and representatively, 'unto righteousness' in Christ their risen head, of whom it is written 'he liveth unto God' (Romans 6:10). We quote below from John Brown's lucid exposition of 1 Peter 2:24.

To be 'dead to sins' is to be delivered from the condemning power of sin; or, in other words, from the condemning sentence of the law, under which, if a man lies, he cannot be holy; and from which, if a man is delivered, his holiness is absolutely secured. To 'live unto righteousness' is plainly just the positive view of that, of which 'to be dead unto sins' is the negative view. 'Righteousness', when opposed to 'sin', in the sense of guilt or liability to punishment, as it very often is in the writings of the apostle Paul, is descriptive of a state of justification. A state of guilt is a state of condemnation by God; a state of righteousness is a state of acceptance with God. To live unto righteousness is in this case to live under the influence of a justified state, a state of acceptance with God; and the apostle's statement is: Christ Jesus, by his sufferings unto death, completely answered the demands of the law on us by bearing away our sins, that we, believing in him, and thereby being united to him, might be as completely freed from our liabilities to punishment, as if we, in our own person, not he himself in his own body, had undergone them; and that we might as really be brought into a state of righteousness, justification, acceptance with God, as if we, not he, in his obedience to death, had magnified the law and made it honourable.

'God sending his own Son in the likeness of sinful flesh, and for sin, condemned sin in the flesh: *that* the righteousness of the law might be fulfilled in us' (Romans 8:3, 4). Here again the *design* of Christ's mission is clearly stated. God sent his Son here in order that (1) the punishment of his peoples' guilt should be inflicted upon their head, (2) that the righteous requirements of the law - perfect obedience - might be met by him for us. This righteousness is said to be 'fulfilled *in* us' because representatively, we were 'in Christ' our Surety: he obeyed the law not only 'for' our good, but so that his obedience should become actually ours by imputation; and thus Christ purchased for us a *title* to heaven.

A parallel passage to Romans 8:3, 4 is found in 2 Corinthians 5:21, 'For he hath made him sin for us, who knew no sin;

that we might be made the righteousness of God in him.' The purpose of Christ's vicarious life and death was that a perfect righteousness should be wrought out for his people and imputed to them by God, so that they might exclaim, '*In the Lord* have I righteousness' (Isaiah 45:24). The righteousness of the believer is wholly *objective*; that is to say, it is something altogether outside of himself. This is clear from the antithesis of 2 Corinthians 5:21. Christ was 'made sin' not inherently, but imputatively, by the guilt of his people being legally transferred to him. In like manner, they are 'made the righteousness of God *in him*', not 'in themselves', by Christ's righteousness being legally reckoned to their account. In the repute of God, Christ and his people constitute one mystical person, hence it is that their sins were imputed to him, and that his righteousness is imputed to them, and therefore we read: 'Christ is the end of the law for righteousness to every one that believeth' (Romans 10:4).

'For Christ also hath once suffered for sins, the just for the unjust, *that* he might bring us to God' (1 Peter 3:18). This wondrous declaration gives us a remarkably clear view of the substitutionary punishment which Christ endured, with the design thereof, namely, to restore his people to priestly nearness and service to God. Four things in it are worthy of our most close attention.

First, Christ 'suffered'. *Sin* was the cause of his suffering. Had there been no sin, Christ had never suffered. To 'suffer' means 'to bear punishment', as in ordinary speech we say, a child suffers for the sins of its parents. Christ suffered for 'us', the whole election of grace: it was for their sin he was penalised.

Second, he suffered 'once'. This must not be understood

to signify that his suffering was confined to the three hours of darkness, but means 'once for all' as in Hebrews 9:27, 28. The 'suffering' which pervaded the whole of Christ's earthly life culminated at the Cross. That suffering was final. His all-sufficient Atonement possesses eternal validity.

Third, Christ himself was personally sinless: it was the 'Just' or 'Righteous' One who suffered. To affirm that he was 'righteous' means that he was approved of God as tested by the standard of the law. He was not only sinless, but one whose life was adjusted to the Divine requirements. As such, he suffered, the pure for the impure, the innocent for the guilty. His sufferings were not on his own account, nor were they from the inevitable course of events or laws of evil in a sinful world; but they were the direct and necessary consequence of his vicariously taking the place of his guilty people. Christ received the punishment they ought to have suffered. He was paid sin's wages which were due them.

Fourth, the end in view of Christ's substitutionary sufferings was to bring his people *to God*. This was only possible by the removal of their sins, which separated them from the thrice Holy One (Isaiah 59:2). By his sufferings, Christ has procured for us access to God. 'But in Christ Jesus ye who sometimes were far off, are *made nigh* by the blood of Christ' (Ephesians 2:13). 'That he might bring us to God' is the most comprehensive expression used in Scripture for stating the design of Christ's Satisfaction. It includes the bringing of his people out of darkness into marvellous light: out of a state of alienation, misery and wrath into one of grace, peace and eternal communion with God. By nature they were in a state of enmity, but Christ has reconciled them by his death (Romans 5:10). By nature they were 'children of wrath'

(Ephesians 2:3), obnoxious to God's judicial displeasure; but by grace they have been accepted into his favour (Romans 5:2). By nature they were spiritual lepers, but by one offering Christ hath 'perfected forever them that are sanctified' (Hebrews 10:14).

Here then, in brief, is the Divine *design* in the Satisfaction of Christ; that God himself might be honoured; that Christ might be glorified; that the elect might be saved by their sins being put away, an abundant life being given them, a perfect righteousness imputed to them, and their being brought into God's favour, presence and fellowship.

CHAPTER 2

The Advent of the Spirit

It is highly important we should closely observe *how* that each of the Eternal Three has been at marked pains to provide for the honour of the other Divine Persons, and we must be as particular to give it to them accordingly. How careful was the Father to duly guard the ineffable glory of the Darling of his bosom when he laid aside the visible insignia of his Deity and took upon him the form of a servant: his voice was then heard more than once proclaiming, 'This is my beloved Son'. How constantly did the incarnate Son divert attention from himself and direct it unto the one who had sent him. In like manner, the Holy Spirit is not here to glorify himself, but rather him whose Vicar and Advocate he is (John 16:14). Blessed is it then to mark how jealous both the Father and the Son have been to safeguard the glory and provide for the honour of the Holy Spirit.

If I go not away, the Comforter will not come' (John 16:7); he will not do these works while I am here, and I have committed all to him. As my Father hath visibly 'committed all judgment unto the Son; that all men should honour the Son, even as they honour the Father' (John 5:22, 23), so I and my Father will send him having committed all these things to him, that all men might honour the Holy Spirit, even as they honour the Father and the Son. Thus wary and careful are every one of the Persons to provide for the honour of each other in our hearts (Thomas Goodwin, 1670).

25

The public advent of the Spirit, for the purpose of ushering in and administering the new covenant, was second in importance only unto the incarnation of our Lord, which was in order to the winding up of the old economy and laying the foundations of the new. When God designed the salvation of his elect, he appointed two great means: the gift of his Son for them, and the gift of his Spirit to them; thereby each of the Persons in the Trinity being glorified. Hence, from the first entrance of sin, there were two great heads to the promises which God gave his people: the sending of his Son to obey and die, the sending of his Spirit to make effectual the fruits of the former. Each of these Divine gifts was bestowed in a manner which suited both to the august Giver himself and the eminent nature of the gifts. Many and marked are the parallels of correspondence between the advent of Christ and the advent of the Spirit.

1. God appointed that there should be a signal coming accorded unto the descent of each from heaven to earth for the performance of the work assigned them. Just as the Son was present with the redeemed Israelites long before his incarnation (Acts 7:37, 38; 1 Corinthians 10:4), yet God decreed for him a visible and more formal advent, which all of his people knew of; so though the Holy Spirit was given to work regeneration in men all through the Old Testament era (Nehemiah 9:20, etc.), and moved the prophets to deliver their messages (2 Peter 1:21), nevertheless God ordained that he should have a coming in state, in a solemn manner, accompanied by visible tokens and glorious effects.

2. Both the advents of Christ and of the Spirit were the subjects of Old Testament prediction. During the past century much has been written upon the Messianic prophecies, but the

promises which God gave concerning the coming of the Holy Spirit constitute a theme which is generally neglected. The following are among the principal pledges which God made that the Spirit should be given unto and poured out upon his saints: Psalm 68:18; Proverbs 1:23; Isaiah 32:15; Ezekiel 36:26, 39:29; Joel 2:28; Haggai 2:9. In them the descent of the Holy Spirit was as definitely announced as was the incarnation of the Saviour in Isaiah 7:14.

3. Just as Christ had John the Baptist to announce his incarnation and to prepare his way, so the Holy Spirit had Christ himself to foretell his coming, and to make ready the hearts of his own for his advent.

4. Just as it was not until 'the fullness of time had come' that God sent forth his Son (Galatians 4:4), so it was not until 'the day of Pentecost was fully come' that God sent forth his Spirit (Acts 2:1).

5. As the Son became incarnate in the holy land, Palestine, so the Spirit descended in Jerusalem.

6. Just as the coming of the Son of God into this world was auspiciously signalised by mighty wonders and signs, so the descent of God the Spirit was attended and attested by stirring displays of Divine power. The advent of each was marked by supernatural phenomena: the angel choir (Luke 2:13) found its counterpart in the 'sound from heaven' (Acts 2:1), and the Shekinah 'glory' (Luke 2:9) in the 'tongues of fire' (Acts 2:3).

7. As an extraordinary star marked the 'house' where the Christ-child was (Matthew 2:9); so a Divine shaking marked the 'house' to which the Spirit had come (Acts 2:2).

8. In connection with the advent of Christ there was both a private and a public aspect to it: in like manner too was it in the giving of the Spirit. The birth of the Saviour was made

known unto a few, but when he was to 'be made manifest to Israel' (John 1:31), he was publicly identified, for at his baptism the heavens were opened, the Spirit descended upon him in the form of a dove, and the voice of the Father audibly owned him as his Son. Correspondingly, the Spirit was communicated to the apostles privately, when the risen Saviour 'breathed on, and said unto them, Receive ye the Holy Spirit' (John 20:22); and later he came publicly on the day of Pentecost when all the great throng then in Jerusalem were made aware of his descent (Acts 2:32-36).

9. The advent of the Son was in order to his becoming incarnate, when the eternal Word was made flesh (John 1:14); so too the advent of the Spirit was in order to his becoming incarnate in Christ's redeemed: as the Saviour had declared to them, the Spirit of truth 'shall be *in* you' (John 14:17). This is a truly marvellous parallel. As the Son of God became man, dwelling in a *human* 'temple' (John 2:19), so the third person of the Trinity took up his abode *in men*, to whom it is said, 'Know ye not that ye are the temple of God, and that the Spirit of God dwelleth in you?' (1 Corinthians 3:16). As the Lord Jesus said to the Father, 'A body hast thou prepared me' (Hebrews 10:5), so the Spirit could say to Christ, 'A body hast thou prepared me' (see Ephesians 2:22).

10. When Christ was born into this world, we are told that Herod 'was *troubled* and all Jerusalem with him' (Matthew 2:3); in like manner, when the Holy Spirit was given we read, 'And there were dwelling at Jerusalem, Jews, devout men out of every nation under heaven. Now when this was noised abroad, the multitude came together, and were *troubled* in mind' (Acts 2:5, 6).

11. It had been predicted that when Christ should appear

he would be unrecognised and unappreciated (Isaiah 53), and so it came to pass; in like manner, the Lord Jesus declared, 'The Spirit of truth, whom the world cannot receive, because it seeth him not, neither knoweth him' (John 14:17).

12. As the Messianic claims of Christ were called into question, so the advent of the Spirit was at once challenged: 'They were all amazed, and *were in doubt*, saying one to another, What meaneth this?' (Acts 2:12).

13. The analogy is yet closer: as Christ was termed 'a winebibber' (Matthew 11:19), so of those filled with the Spirit it was said, 'These men are full of new wine' (Acts 2:13)!

14. As the public advent of Christ was heralded by John the Baptist (John 1:29), so the meaning of the public descent of the Spirit was interpreted by Peter (Acts 2:15-36).

15. God appointed unto Christ the executing of a stupendous work, even that of purchasing the redemption of his people; even so to the Spirit has been assigned the momentous task of effectually applying to his elect the virtues and benefits of the atonement.

16. As in the discharge of his work the Son honoured the Father (John 14:10), so in the fulfilment of his mission the Spirit glorifies the Son (John 16:13, 14).

17. As the Father paid holy deference unto the Son by bidding the disciples, 'Hear ye him' (Matthew 17:5), in like manner the Son shows respect for his Paraclete by saying, 'He that hath an ear, let him *hear what the Spirit saith* unto the churches' (Revelation 2:7).

18. As Christ committed his saints into the safekeeping of the Holy Spirit (John 16:7; 14:16), so the Spirit will yet deliver up those saints unto Christ, as the word 'receive' in John 14:3

plainly implies. We trust that the reader will find the same
spiritual delight in perusing this chapter as the writer had in
preparing it.

At Pentecost the Holy Spirit came as he had never come
before. Something then transpired which inaugurated a new
era for the world, a new power for righteousness, a new basis
for fellowship. On that day the fearing Peter was transformed
into the intrepid evangelist. On that day the new wine of
Christianity burst the old bottles of Judaism, and the Word
went forth in a multiplicity of Gentile tongues. On that day
more souls seem to have been truly regenerated, than during
all the three and one half years of Christ's public ministry.
What had happened? It is not enough to say that the Spirit of
God was given, for he had been given long before, both to
individuals and the nation of Israel (Nehemiah 9:20; Haggai
2:5); no, the pressing question is, *In what sense* was he then
given? This leads us to carefully consider the *meaning* of the
Spirit's advent.

1. It was the fulfilment of the Divine promise.
First, of the Father himself. During the Old Testament
dispensation, he declared, again and again, that he would pour
out the Spirit upon his people (see Proverbs 1:23; Isaiah
32:15; Joel 2:28, etc.); and now these gracious declarations
were accomplished.

Second, of John the Baptist. When he was stirring the
hearts of the multitudes by his call to repentance and his
demand of baptism, many thought he must be the long-
expected Messiah, but he declared unto them, 'I indeed
baptize you with water, but one mightier than I cometh, the
latchet of whose shoes I am not worthy to unloose: *he* shall

baptise you *with the Holy Spirit and with fire*' (Luke 3:15, 16). Accordingly he did so on the day of Pentecost, as Acts 2:32, 33 plainly shows.

Third, of Christ. Seven times over the Lord Jesus avowed that he would give or send the Holy Spirit: Luke 24:49; John 7:37-39; 14:16-19; 14:26; 15:26; 16:7; Acts 1:5, 8. From these we may particularly notice, 'When the Comforter is come, whom *I will send* unto you from the Father... he shall testify of me' (John 15:26): 'It is expedient for you that I go away; for if I go not away, the Comforter will not come unto you; but if I depart, *I will send him* unto you' (John 16:7). That which took place in John 20:22 and in Acts 2 was the fulfilment of those promises. In them we behold the faith of the Mediator: he had appropriated the promise which the Father had given him, 'Therefore being by the right hand of God exalted, and having received of the Father the promise of the Holy Spirit, *he* hath shed forth this, which ye now see and hear' (Acts 2:33) - it was by faith's anticipation the Lord spoke as he did in the above passage.

The Holy Spirit was God's ascension gift to Christ, that he might be bestowed by Christ, as his ascension gift to the church. Hence Christ had said, 'Behold, I send the promise of my Father upon you.' This was the promised gift of the Father to the Son, and the Saviour's promised gift to his believing people. How easy now to reconcile the apparent contradiction of Christ's earlier and later words: 'I will pray the Father and *he shall give you* another Comforter'; and then, afterward, 'If I depart, *I will send him* unto you.' The Spirit was the Father's answer to the prayer of the Son; and so the gift was transferred by him to the mystical body of which he is the head (A T Pierson in *The Acts of the Holy Spirit*).

2. It was the fulfilment of an important Old Testament type.
It is this which explains to us why the Spirit was given on the
day of 'Pentecost', which was one of the principal religious
feasts of Israel. Just as there was a profound significance to
Christ's dying on Passover Day (giving us the antitype of
Exodus 12), so there was in the coming of the Spirit on the
fiftieth day after Christ's resurrection. The type is recorded in
Leviticus 23, to which we can here make only the briefest
allusion. In Leviticus 23:4 we read, 'These are the feasts of the
Lord.' The first of them is the Passover (v 5) and the second
'unleavened bread' (v 6 etc.). The two together speaking of
the sinless Christ offering himself as a sacrifice for the sins of
his people. The third is the 'wave sheaf' (v 10 etc.) which was
the 'firstfruits of the harvest' (v 10), presented to God 'on the
morrow after the (Jewish) Sabbath' (v 11), a figure of Christ's
resurrection (1 Corinthians 15:23).

The fourth is the feast of 'weeks' (see Exodus 34:22;
Deuteronomy 16:10, 16) so-called because of the seven
complete weeks of Leviticus 23:15; also known as 'Pentecost' (which means 'Fiftieth) because of the 'fifty days' of
Leviticus 23:16. It was then the balance of the harvest *began*
to be gathered in. On that day Israel was required to present
unto God 'two wave loaves', which were also designated 'the
first-fruits unto the Lord' (Leviticus 23:17). The antitype of
which was the saving of the three thousand on the day of
Pentecost: the 'firstfruits' of Christ's atonement (compare
James 1:18). The first loaf represented those redeemed from
among the Jews, the second loaf was *anticipatory* and pointed
to the gathering in of God's elect from among the Gentiles,
begun in Acts 10.

3. It was the beginning of a new dispensation.

This was plainly intimated in the type of Leviticus 23, for on
the day of Pentecost Israel was definitely required to offer a
'*new* meal offering unto the Lord' (v 16). Still more clearly
was it foreannounced in a yet more important and significant
type, namely, that of the beginning of the Mosaic economy,
which took place only when the nation of Israel formally
entered into covenant relationship with Jehovah at Sinai. Now
it is exceedingly striking to observe that just *fifty days* elapsed
from the time when the Hebrews emerged from the house of
bondage till they received the law from the mouth of Moses.
They left Egypt on the fifteenth of the first month (Numbers
33:3), and arrived at Sinai on the first of the third month
(Exodus 19:1, note 'the same day'), which would be the forty-
sixth. The next day Moses went up into the mount, and three
days later the law was delivered (Exodus 19:11)! And just as
there was a period of fifty days from Israel's deliverance from
Egypt until the beginning of the Mosaic economy, so the same
length of time followed the resurrection of Christ (when his
people were delivered from hell) to the beginning of the
Christian economy!

That a new dispensation commenced at Pentecost further
appears from the 'tongues like as *of fire*' (Acts 2:1). When
John the Baptist announced that Christ would baptise 'with
the Holy Spirit and with fire', the last words might have
suggested material burning to any people except Jews, but in
their minds far other thoughts would be awakened. To them
it would recall the scene when their great progenitor asked the
God who promised he should inherit that land wherein he was
a stranger, 'Lord, GOD *whereby shall I know* that I shall inherit
it?' The answer was, 'Behold a smoking furnace and a burning

lamp...' (Genesis 15:17). It would recall the fire which Moses saw in the burning bush. It would recall the 'pillar of fire' which guided by night, and the Shekinah which descended and filled the tabernacle. Thus, in the promise of baptism by fire, they would at once recognise the approach of *a new manifestation of the presence and power of God*!

Again, when we read that 'there appeared unto them cloven tongues like as of fire, and it sat upon each of them' (Acts 2:2), further evidence is found that a new dispensation had now commenced.

The word, *sat*, in Scripture marks *an ending and a beginning*. The process of preparation is ended and the established order has begun. It marks the end of creation and the beginning of normal forces. 'In six days the Lord made heaven and earth, the sea, and all that in them is, and rested the seventh day.' There is no weariness in God. He did not rest from fatigue: what it means is that all creative work was accomplished. The same figure is used of the Redeemer. Of him it is said 'when he had made purification for sins (he) *sat down* on the right hand of the Majesty on high'. No other priesthood had sat down. The priests of the Temple ministered standing because their ministry was provisional and preparatory, a parable and a prophecy. Christ's own ministry was part of the preparation for the coming of the Spirit. Until he 'sat down' in glory, there could be no dispensation of the Spirit... When the work of redemption was complete, the Spirit was given, and when he came he *sat*. He reigns in the Church as Christ reigns in the heavens.

There are few incidents more illuminating than that recorded in 'the last day of the feast' in John 7:37-39. The feast was that of Tabernacles. The feast proper lasted seven days, during which all Israel dwelt in booths. Special sacrifices were offered and special rites observed. Every morning one of the priests brought water from the pool of Siloam, and amidst the sounding of trumpets and other demonstrations of joy, the water was poured upon the altar. The rite was a celebration and a prophecy. It commemorated the miraculous supply of water in the wilderness, and it bore witness to the expectation of the coming of the Spirit. On the seventh day the ceremony of the poured water ceased, but the eighth was a day of holy convocation, the greatest day of all.

On that day there was no water poured upon the altar, and it was on the waterless day that Jesus stood on the spot and cried, saying: 'If any man thirst, let him come unto me and drink.' Then he added those words: 'He that believeth on me, as the scripture has said, from within him shall flow rivers of living water.' The apostle adds the interpretative comment: 'But this spake he of the Spirit, which they that believe on him were to receive: for the Spirit was not given because Jesus was not yet glorified.'

'As the scripture hath said.' There is no such passage in the Scripture as that quoted, but the prophetic part of the water ceremony was based upon certain Old Testament symbols and prophecies in which water flowed forth from Zion to cleanse, renew, and fructify the world. A study of Joel 3:18 and Ezekiel 47 will supply the key to the meaning both of the rite and our Lord's promise. The Holy Spirit was 'not yet given', but he was promised, and his coming should be from the place of blood, the altar of sacrifice. Calvary opened the fountain from which poured forth the blessing of Pentecost (Samuel Chadwick *The Way to Pentecost*)).

We have considered *the meaning* of the Spirit's descent, and pointed out that it was the fulfilment of Divine promise, the accomplishment of Old Testament types, and the beginning of a new dispensation. It was also *the Grace of God flowing unto the Gentiles*. But first let us observe and admire the marvellous grace of God extended unto the Jews themselves. In his charge to the apostles, the Lord Jesus gave orders that 'repentance and remission of sins should be preached in his name among all nations, *beginning at Jerusalem*' (Luke 24:47), not because the Jews had any longer a covenant standing before God - for the Nation was abandoned by him

before the crucifixion - see Matthew 23:38 - but in order to
display his matchless mercy and sovereign benignity. Accordingly, in the Acts we see his love shining forth in the midst
of the rebellious city. In the very place where the Lord Jesus
had been slain the full gospel was now preached, and three
thousand were quickened by the Holy Spirit.

But the gospel was to be restricted to the Jews no longer.
Though the apostles were to commence their testimony in
Jerusalem, yet Christ's glorious and all-efficacious Name was
to be proclaimed 'among all nations'. The earnest of this was
given when 'devout men out of every nation under heaven'
(Acts 2:5) exclaimed, 'How hear we every man in his own
tongue?' (v 8). It was an entirely new thing. What occurred in
Acts 2 was a part reversal and in blessed contrast from what
is recorded in Genesis 11. There we find 'the tongues were
divided to destroy an *evil* unity, and to show God's holy hatred
of Babel's iniquity. In Acts 2 we have grace at Jerusalem, and
a new and precious unity, suggestive of another building
(Matthew 16:18), with living *stones* - contrast the 'bricks' of
Genesis 11:3 and its tower' (P W Heward). In Genesis 11 the
dividing of tongues was *in judgment*; in Acts 2 the cloven
tongues was *in grace*; and in Revelation 7:9, 10 we see men
of all tongues *in glory*.

We next consider *the purpose* of the Spirit's descent.

1. To witness unto Christ's exaltation.

Pentecost was God's seal upon the Messiahship of Jesus. In
proof of his pleasure in and acceptance of the sacrificial work
of his Son, God raised him from the dead, exalted him to his
own right hand, and gave him the Spirit to bestow upon his
Church (Acts 2:33). It has been beautifully pointed out by

another that, on the hem of the ephod worn by the high priest of Israel were golden bells and pomegranates (Exodus 28:33, 34). The sound of the bells (and that which gave them sound was their *tongues*) furnished evidence that he was alive while serving in the sanctuary. The high priest was a type of Christ (Hebrews 8:1); the holy place was a figure of heaven (Hebrews 9:24); the 'sound from heaven' and the speaking 'in tongues' (Acts 2:2, 4) were a witness that our Lord was alive in heaven, ministering there as the High Priest of his people.

2. To take Christ's place.

This is clear from his own words to the apostles, 'And I will pray the Father, and he shall give you another Comforter, that he may abide with you forever' (John 14:16). Until then, Christ had been their 'Comforter', but he was soon to return to heaven; nevertheless, as he went on to assure them, 'I will not leave you orphans, I will come to you' (marginal rendering of John 14:18); he did 'come' to them corporately after his resurrection, but he 'came' to them spiritually and abidingly in the person of his Deputy on the day of Pentecost. The Spirit, then, fills the place on earth of our absent Lord in heaven, with this additional advantage, that, during the days of his flesh the Saviour's body confined him unto one location, whereas the Holy Spirit - not having assumed a body as the mode of his incarnation - is equally and everywhere resident in and abiding with every believer.

3. To further Christ's Cause.

This is plain from his declaration concerning the Comforter: 'He shall glorify me' (John 16:14). The word 'Paraclete' (translated 'Comforter' all through the gospel) is also ren-

dered 'Advocate' in 1 John 2:1, and an 'advocate' is one who
appears as *the representative* of another. The Holy Spirit is
here to interpret and vindicate Christ, to administer for Christ
in his Church and Kingdom. He is here to accomplish his
redeeming purpose in the world. He fills the mystical Body of
Christ, directing its movements, controlling its members,
inspiring its wisdom, supplying its strength. The Holy Spirit
becomes to the believer individually and the church collec-
tively all that Christ would have been had he remained on
earth. Moreover, he seeks out each one of those for whom
Christ died, quickens them into newness of life, convicts them
of sin, gives them faith to lay hold of Christ, and causes them
to grow in grace and become fruitful.

It is important to see that the mission of the Spirit is for the
purpose of continuing and completing that of Christ's. The
Lord Jesus declared, 'I am come to send fire on the earth: and
what will I, if it be already kindled? But I have a baptism to
be baptised with; and how am I straitened till it be accomplished!' (Luke 12:49, 50). The preaching of the gospel was
to be like 'fire on the earth', giving light and warmth to human
hearts; it was 'kindled' then, but would spread much more
rapidly later. Until his death Christ was 'straitened': it did not
consist with God's purpose for the gospel to be preached more
openly and extensively; but after Christ's resurrection, it went
forth unto all nations. Following the ascension, Christ was no
longer 'straitened' and the Spirit was poured forth in the
plenitude of his power.

4. To endue Christ's servants.
'Tarry ye in Jerusalem until ye be endued with power from on
high' (Luke 24:49) had been the word of Christ to his apostles.

Sufficient for the disciple to be as his Master. *He* had waited, waited till he was thirty, ere he was 'anointed to preach good tidings' (Isaiah 61:1). The servant is not above his Lord: if he was indebted to the Spirit for the power of his ministry, the apostles must not attempt their work without the Spirit's unction. Accordingly they waited, and the Spirit came upon them. All was changed: boldness supplanted fear, strength came instead of weakness, ignorance gave place to wisdom, and mighty wonders were wrought through them.

Unto the apostles whom he had chosen, the risen Saviour 'commanded them that they should not depart from Jerusalem, but wait for the promise of the Father', assuring them that 'Ye shall receive power after that the Holy Spirit is come unto you; and ye shall be witnesses unto me both in Jerusalem and in all Samaria, and unto the uttermost parts of the earth' (Acts 1:2, 4, 8). Accordingly, we read that, 'And when the day of Pentecost was fully come, they were all with one accord in one place' (Acts 2:1): their unity of mind evidently looked back to the Lord's command and promise, and their trustful expectancy of the fulfilment thereof. The Jewish 'day' was from sunset unto the following sunset, and as what took place here in Acts 2 occurred during the early hours of the morning - probably soon after sunrise - we are told that the day of Pentecost was 'fully come'.

The outward marks of the Spirit's advent were three in number: the 'sound from heaven as of a rushing mighty wind', the 'cloven tongues as of fire', and the speaking 'with other tongues as the Spirit gave them utterance'. Concerning the precise signification of these phenomena, and the practical bearing of them on us today, there has been wide difference of opinion, especially since the beginning of this century.

Inasmuch as God himself has not seen fit to furnish us with a full and detailed explanation of them, it behoves all interpreters to speak with reserve and reverence. According to our own measure of light, we shall endeavour briefly to point out some of those things which appear to be most obvious.

First, the 'rushing mighty wind' which filled all the house was the *collective* sign, in which, apparently, all the hundred and twenty of Acts 1:15 shared. This was an emblem of the invincible energy with which the Third Person of the Trinity works upon the hearts of men, bearing down all opposition before him, in a manner which cannot be explained (John 3:8), but which is at once apparent by the effects produced. Just as the course of a hurricane may be clearly traced after it has passed, so the transforming work of the Spirit in regeneration is made unmistakably manifest unto all who have eyes to see spiritual things.

Second, 'there appeared unto them cloven tongues like as of fire, and it sat upon each of them' (Acts 2:3), that is, upon the Twelve, and upon them alone. The proof of this is conclusive. First, it was to the apostles only that the Lord spoke in Luke 24:49. Second, to them only did he, by the Spirit, give commandments after his resurrection (Acts 1:2). Third, to them only did he give the promise of Acts 1:8. Fourth, at the end of Acts 1 we read 'he (Matthias) was numbered with *the eleven* apostles'. Acts 2 opens with 'And' connecting it with 1:26 and says, 'they (the twelve) were all with one accord in one place' and on *them* the Spirit now 'sat' (Acts 2:3). Fifth, when the astonished multitude came together they exclaimed, 'Are not *all* these which speak *Galileans*?' (Acts 2:7), namely, the 'men' (Greek, 'males') *of Galilee*' of 1:11! Sixth, in Acts 2:14, 15 we read, 'But Peter standing up *with the eleven* lifted up his voice and said to them, Ye men of Galilee and all ye that dwell in Judaea, be this known unto you and hearken unto my words: For *these* are not drunk' - the word 'these' can only refer to the 'eleven' standing up with Peter!

These 'cloven tongues like as of fire' which descended upon the apostles was the *individual* sign, the Divine credential that they were the authorised ambassadors of the enthroned Lamb. The baptism of the Holy Spirit was a baptism of *fire*.

> Our God is a consuming fire. The elect sign of his presence is the fire unkindled of earth, and the chosen symbol of his approval is the sacred flame: covenant and sacrifice, sanctuary and dispensation were sanctified and approved by the descent of fire. 'The God that answereth by fire, he is the God' (1 Kings 18:24). That is the final and universal test of Deity. Jesus Christ came to bring fire on the earth. The symbol of Christianity is not a Cross, but a Tongue of Fire (Samuel Chadwick).

Third, the apostles 'speaking with other tongues' was the *public* sign. 1 Corinthians 14:22 declares 'tongues are for a sign, not to them that believe, but to them that believe not', and as the previous verse (where Isaiah 28:11 is quoted) so plainly shows, they were a sign unto *unbelieving Israel*. A striking illustration and proof of this is found in Acts 11, where Peter sought to convince his sceptical brethren in Jerusalem that God's grace was now flowing forth unto the Gentiles; it was his description of the Holy Spirit's falling upon Cornelius and his household (Acts 11:15-18 and cf. 10:45, 46) which convinced them. It is highly significant that the Pentecostal type of Leviticus 23:22 divided the harvest into three degrees and stages: the 'reaping' or *main* part, corresponding to Acts 2 at Jerusalem; the 'corners of the field' corresponding to Acts

10 at 'Caesarea Philippi' which was in the corner of Palestine; and the 'gleaning' for 'the stranger' corresponding to Acts 19 at Gentile Ephesus! These were the only three occasions of 'tongues' recorded in Acts.

It is well known to some of our readers that during the last generation many earnest souls have been deeply exercised by what is known as 'the Pentecostal movement' and the question is frequently raised as to whether or not the strange power displayed in their meetings, issuing in unintelligible sounds called 'tongues', is the genuine gift of the Spirit. Those who have joined the movement - some of them godly souls, we believe - insist that not only is the gift genuine, but it is the duty of all Christians to seek the same. But surely such seem to overlook the fact that it was not any *unknown* tongue' which was spoken by the apostles: foreigners who heard them had no difficulty in understanding what was said (Acts 2:8).

If what has just been said be not sufficient, then let our appeal be unto 2 Timothy 3:16, 17. God has now *fully* revealed his mind to us: all that we need to '*thoroughly* furnish' us 'unto *all* good works' is already in our hands! Personally the writer would not take the trouble to walk into the next room to hear any person deliver a message which he claimed was inspired by the Holy Spirit; with the *completed* Scriptures in our possession, nothing more is required except for the Spirit to interpret and apply them. Let it also be duly observed that there is not a single exhortation in all the Epistles of the New Testament that the saints should seek 'a fresh Pentecost', no, not even to the carnal Corinthians or the legal Galatians.

As a sample of what was believed by the early 'fathers' we quote the following:

Augustine saith, Miracles were once necessary to make the world believe the gospel, but he who now seeks a sign that he may believe is a wonder, yea a monster.' Chrysostom concludeth upon the same grounds that, 'There is now in the Church no necessity of working miracles', and calls him a 'false prophet' who now takes in hand to work them (William Perkins, 1604).

In Acts 2:16 we find Peter was moved by God to give a general explanation of the great wonders which had just taken place. Jerusalem was, at this time of the feast, filled with a great concourse of people. The sudden sound from heaven 'as of a rushing mighty wind', filling the house where the apostles were gathered together, soon drew thither a multitude of people; and as they, in wonderment, heard the apostles speak in their own varied languages, they asked, 'What meaneth *this*?' (Acts 2:12). Peter then declared, '*This* is that which was spoken of by the prophet Joel.' The prophecy given by Joel (2:28-32) now began to receive its fulfilment, the latter part of which we believe is to be understood symbolically.

And what is the bearing of all this upon us today? We will reply in a single sentence: the advent of the Spirit *followed the exaltation of Christ*: if then we desire to enjoy more of the Spirit's power and blessing, we must give Christ the throne of our hearts and crown him the Lord of our lives.

CHAPTER 3

The Spirit Assuring

We do not propose to treat of the Spirit assuring in a topical and general way, but to confine ourselves to his inspiring the Christian with a sense of his adoption into the family of God, limiting ourselves to two or three particular passages which treat specifically thereof. In Romans 8:15 we read, 'For ye have not received the spirit of bondage again to fear; but ye have received the Spirit of adoption, whereby we cry, Abba, Father.' The eighth chapter of Romans has ever been a great favourite with the Lord's people, for it contains a wide variety of cordials for their encouragement and strengthening in the running of that heavenly race which is marked out and set before them in the Word of God. The apostle is there writing to such as have been brought, by the grace and power of the Holy Spirit, to know and believe on the Lord Jesus, and who by their communion with him are led to set their affection upon things above.

First, let us observe that Romans 8:15 opens with the word, 'For,' which not only suggests a close connection with that which precedes, but intimates that a proof is now furnished of what had just been affirmed. In verse 12, the apostle had said, 'Therefore, brethren, we are debtors, not to the flesh, to live after the flesh': the 'Therefore' being a conclusion drawn from all the considerations set forth in verses 1-11. Next, the apostle had declared, 'For if ye live after the flesh, ye shall die:

44

but if ye through the Spirit do mortify the deeds of the body, ye shall live' (v 13); which means, first, ye shall *continue* to 'live' a life of *grace* now; and second, this shall be followed by a 'life' of *glory* throughout eternity. Then the apostle added, 'For as many as are led by the Spirit of God, they are the sons of God' (v 14), which is a confirmation and amplification of verse 13: none live a life of grace save those who are 'led by the Spirit of God' - are inwardly controlled and outwardly governed by him: for they only are 'the sons of God'.

Delivered from bondage

Now, in verse 15, the apostle both amplifies and confirms what he had said in verse 14: there he shows the reality of that relationship with God which our regeneration makes manifest - obedient subjection to him as dear children; here he brings before us further proof of our Divine sonship - deliverance from a servile fear, the exercise of a filial confidence. Let us consider the negative first: 'For ye have not received the spirit of bondage again to fear.' By nature we were in 'bondage' to sin, to Satan, to the world; yet they did not work in us a spirit of 'fear', so they cannot be (as some have supposed) what the apostle had reference to: rather is it what the Spirit's convicting us of sin wrought in us. When he applies the law to the conscience our complacency is shattered, our false peace is destroyed, and we are terrified at the thought of God's righteous wrath and the prospect of eternal punishment.

When a soul has received life and light from the Spirit of God, so that he perceives the infinite enormity and filthiness of sin, and the total depravity and corruption of every faculty of his soul and body, that spirit of *legality* which is in all men by nature, is at once stirred up and alarmed, so that the mind is possessed with secret doubts and suspicions of God's mercy in Christ to save; and thereby the soul is brought into a state of legal bondage and fear. When a soul is first awakened by the Holy Spirit, it is subject to a variety of fears; yet it does not follow from thence that *he* works those fears or is the author of them: rather are they to be ascribed to our own unbelief. When the Spirit is pleased to convict of sin and gives the conscience to feel the guilt of it, it is to show the sinner his need of *Christ*, and not to drive him unto despair.

No doubt there is also a dispensational allusion in the passage we are now considering. During the Mosaic economy, believing Israelites were to a considerable extent under the spirit of legal bondage, because the sacrifices and ablutions of the Levitical institutions could not take away sins. The precepts of the ceremonial law were so numerous, so various, so burdensome, that the Jews were kept in perpetual bondage. Hence, we find Peter referring to the same as 'a yoke which neither our fathers nor we were able to bear' (Acts 15:10). Much under the Old Testament dispensation tended to a legal spirit. But believers, under the gospel, are favoured with a clearer, fuller, and more glorious display and revelation of God's grace in the person and work of the Lord Jesus Christ, the evangel making known the design and sufficiency of his finished work, so that full provision is now made to deliver them from all servile fear.

An eternal relationship

Turning now to the positive side: believers have 'received the Spirit of adoption, whereby they cry, Abba, Father': they have received that unspeakable Gift which attests and makes known to them their adoption by God. Before the foundation of the world God predestinated them 'unto the adoption of children by Jesus Christ to himself' (Ephesians 1:5). But more: the elect were not only predestinated *unto* the adoption of children - to actually and openly enjoy this inestimable favour in time - but this blessing was itself provided and bestowed upon them in the Everlasting Covenant of grace, in which they not only had promise of this relationship, but were given in that covenant to Christ under that very character. Therefore does the Lord Jesus say, 'Behold I and the children which God hath given me' (Hebrews 2:13).

It is to be carefully noted that God's elect are spoken of as 'children' *previous to* the Holy Spirit's being sent into their hearts: 'Because ye *are* sons, God hath sent forth the Spirit of his Son into your hearts' (Galatians 4:6). They are not, then, made children by the new birth. They were 'children' before Christ died for them: 'he prophesied that Jesus should die for that nation; and not for that nation only, but that also he should gather together in one *the children* of God that were scattered abroad' (John 11:51, 52). They were not, then, made children by what Christ did for them. Yea, they were 'children' before the Lord Jesus became incarnate: 'Forasmuch then as *the children* are partakers of flesh and blood, he also himself likewise took part of the same' (Hebrews 2:14). Thus it is a great mistake to confound adoption and regeneration: they are two distinct things; the latter being both the effect and evidence of the former. Adoption was by an act of God's will in eternity; regeneration is by the work of his grace in time.

Had there been no adoption, there would be no regeneration: yet the former is not complete without the latter. By adoption the elect were put into *the relation* of children; by regeneration they are given *a nature* suited to that relation. So

high is the honour of being taken into the family of God, and
so wondrous is the privilege of having God for our Father, that
some extraordinary benefit is needed by us to assure our hearts
of the same. This we have when we receive the Spirit of
adoption. For God to give us his Spirit is far more than if he
had given us all the world, for the latter would be something
outside himself, whereas the former *is* himself. The death of
Christ on the cross was a demonstration of God's love for his
people, yet that was done without them; but in connection
with what we are now considering 'the love of God is shed
abroad *in our hearts* by the Holy Spirit which is given unto us'
(Romans 5:5).

It is a wondrous and blessed fact that God manifests his
love to the members of his Church in precisely the same way
that he evidenced his love to its head when he became
incarnate, namely, by the transcendent gift of his Spirit. The
Spirit came upon Jesus Christ as the proof of God's love to
him and also as the visible demonstration of his Sonship. The
Spirit of God descended like a dove and abode upon him, and
then the Father's voice was heard saying, 'This is my beloved
Son, in whom I am well pleased' (compare John 3:34, 35). In
fulfilment of Christ's prayer, 'I have declared to them thy
name, and will declare it; that the love wherewith thou hast
loved me may be *in them*' (John 17:26), the Spirit is given to
his redeemed, to signify the sameness of the Father's love to
his Son and to his sons. Thus, the inhabitation of the Spirit in
the Christian is both the surest sign of God's fatherly love and
the proof of his adoption.

'Because ye are sons, God hath sent forth the Spirit of his
Son into your hearts, crying, Abba, Father' (Galatians 4:6).
Because they had been eternally predestinated unto the adop-

tion of sons (Ephesians 1:4, 5); because they were actually
given to Christ under that character in the Everlasting Covenant (John 11:52; Hebrews 2:13), at God's appointed time
the Holy Spirit is sent into their hearts to give them a
knowledge of the wondrous fact that they have a place in the
very family of God and that God is their Father. This it is
which inclines their hearts to love him, delight in him, and
place all their dependence on him. The great design of the
gospel is to reveal the love of God to his people, and thereby
recover their love to God, that they may love him again who
first loved them. But the bare revelation of that love in the
Word will not secure this, until 'the love of God is shed abroad
in our hearts by the Holy Spirit which is given unto us'
(Romans 5:5).

It is by the gracious work of the Holy Spirit that the elect
are recovered from the flesh and the world unto God. By
nature they love themselves and the world above God; but the
Holy Spirit imparts to them a new nature, and himself
indwells them, so that they now love God and live to him. This
it is which prepares them to believe and appropriate the
gospel. The effects of the Spirit's entering as the Spirit of
adoption are liberty, confidence and holy delight. As they had
'received' from the first Adam 'the spirit of bondage' - a
legalistic spirit which produced 'fear', their receiving the
Spirit of adoption is all the more grateful: liberty being the
sweeter because of the former captivity. The law having done
its work in the conscience, they can now appreciate the glad
tidings of the gospel - the revelation of the amazing love and
grace of God in Jesus Christ. A spirit of love is now bred in
them by the knowledge of the same.

A filial spirit

The blessed fruit of receiving the Spirit of adoption is that
there is born in them a childlike affection towards God and a
childlike confidence in him: 'Whereby we cry, Abba, Father.'
The apostle employs in the original two different languages.
'Abba', being Syrian, and 'Father' being Greek, the one
familiar to the Jews, the other to the Gentiles. By so doing he
denotes that believing Jews and Gentiles are children of one
family, alike privileged to approach God as their Father.

Christ, our peace, having broken down the middle wall of partition
between them; and now, at the same mercy seat, the Christian Jew and
the believing Gentile, both one in Christ Jesus, *meet*, as the rays of light
converge and blend in one common centre - at the feet of the reconciled
Father (Octavius Winslow).

As the Spirit of adoption, the Holy Spirit bestows upon the
quickened soul a filial spirit: he acts in unison with the Son and
gives a sense of our relationship as sons. Emancipating from
that bondage and fear which the application of the law stirred
up within us, he brings us into the joyous liberty which the
reception of the gospel bestows. O the blessedness of being
delivered from the Covenant of Works! O the bliss of reading
our sentence of pardon in the blood of Immanuel! It is by virtue
of our having received the Spirit of adoption that we cry 'Father!
Father!' It is the cry of our own heart, the desire of our soul going
out to God. And yet *our* spirit does not originate it: without the
immediate presence, operation and grace of the Holy Spirit we
neither would nor could know God as our 'Father'. The Spirit
is the Author of everything in us which goes out after God.

This filial spirit which the Christian has received is evidenced in various ways. First, by a *holy reverence* for God our

Father, as the natural child should honour or reverence his human parent. Second, by *confidence* in God our Father, as the natural child trusts in and relies upon his earthly parent. Third, by *love* for our Father, as the natural child has an affectionate regard for his parent. Fourth, by *subjection to* God our Father, as the natural child obeys his parent. This filial spirit prompts him to approach God with *spiritual freedom*, so that he clings to him with the confidence of a babe, and leans upon him with the calm repose of a little one lying on its parent's breast. It admits to the closest intimacy. To God *as his 'Father'* the Christian should repair at all times, casting all his care upon him, knowing that he careth for him (1 Peter 5:7). It is to be manifested by an affectionate subjection (obedience) to him 'as dear children' (Ephesians 5:1).

The Spirit of adoption is the Spirit of God, who proceedeth from the Father and the Son, and who is sent by them to shed abroad the love of God in the heart, to give a real enjoyment of it, and to fill the soul with joy and peace in believing. He comes to testify of Christ; and by taking of the things which are his, and showing them to his people, he draws their heart to him; and by opening unto them the freeness and fullness of Divine grace, and the exceeding great and precious promises which God has given unto his people, he leads them to know their interest in Christ; and helps them in his name, blood, and righteousness, to approach their heavenly Father with holy delight (S E Pierce).

John Gill observes that the word 'Abba' reads backwards the same as forwards, implying that God is the Father of his people in adversity as well as prosperity. The Christian's is an inalienable relationship: God is as much his 'Father' when he chastens as when he delights, as much so when he frowns as when he smiles. God will never disown his own children or disinherit them as heirs. When Christ taught his disciples to

pray he bade them approach the mercy seat and say, 'Our
Father which art in heaven'. He himself, in Gethsemane,
cried, 'Abba, Father' (Mark 14:36) - expressive of his confidence in and dependency upon him. To address God as
'Father' encourages faith, confirms hope, warms the heart,
and draws out its affections to him who is Love itself.

Let it next be pointed out that this filial spirit is subject to
the state and place in which the Christian yet is. Some suppose
that if we have received the Spirit of adoption there must be
produced a steady and uniform assurance, a perpetual fire
burning upon the altar of the heart. Not so. When the Son of
God became incarnate, he condescended to yield unto all the
sinless infirmities of human nature, so that he hungered and
ate, wearied and slept. In like manner, the Holy Spirit deigns
to submit himself to the laws and circumstances which
ordinarily regulate human nature. In heaven the man Christ
Jesus is glorified; and in heaven the Spirit in the Christian will
shine like a perpetual star. But on earth, he indwells our hearts
like a flickering flame; never to be extinguished, but not
always bright, and needing to be guarded from rude blasts, or
why bid us 'quench not the Spirit' (1 Thessalonians 5:19)?

The Spirit, then, does not grant the believer assurance
irrespective of his own carefulness and diligence. 'Let your
loins be girded, your lights *burning*' (Luke 12:35): the latter
being largely determined by the former. The Christian is not
always in the enjoyment of a childlike confidence. And why?
Because he is often guilty of 'grieving' the Spirit, and then he
withholds much of his comfort. Hereby we may ascertain our
communion with God and when it is interrupted, when he be
pleased or displeased with us - by the motions or withdrawings
of the Spirit's consolation. Note the order in Acts 9:31,

'Walking in the fear of the Lord and in the comfort of the Holy Spirit'; and again in Acts 11:24, 'he was a good man and full of the Holy Spirit'. Hence, when our confidence toward 'the Father' is clouded, we should search our ways and find out what is the matter.

Empty professors are fatally deluded by a false *confidence*, a complacent taking for granted that they are real Christians when they have never been born again. But many true possessors are plagued by a *false diffidence*, a doubting whether they be Christians at all. None are so inextricably caught in the toils of a false confidence as they who suspect not their delusion and are unconscious of their imminent danger. On the other hand, none are so far away from that false confidence as those who tremble lest *they* be cherishing it. True diffidence is a distrust of *myself*. True confidence is a leaning wholly upon *Christ*, and *that* is ever accompanied by utter renunciation of myself. Self-renunciation is the heartfelt acknowledgment that my resolutions, best efforts, faith and holiness, are nothing before God, and that Christ must be my All.

In all genuine Christians there is a co-mingling of real confidence and false diffidence, because as long as they remain on this earth there is in them the root of faith and the root of doubt. Hence their prayer is, 'Lord, I believe; help thou mine unbelief' (Mark 9:24). In some Christians *faith* prevails more than it does in others; in some *unbelief* is more active than in others. Therefore some have a stronger and steadier assurance than others. The presence of the indwelling Spirit is largely evidenced by our frequent recourse to the Father in prayer - often with sighs, sobs, and groans. The consciousness of the Spirit of adoption within us is largely regulated by the extent to which we yield ourselves to his government.

CHAPTER 4

The Necessity of Spiritual Growth

None can possibly make any progress in the Christian life unless he first be a Christian. It is indeed striking to note that this title is used by the Holy Spirit in a *twofold* way: primarily it signifies an 'anointed one'; subordinately it denotes a 'disciple of Christ'. Thereby there are brought together in a truly wonderful manner both the Divine and the human sides. Our 'anointing' with the Spirit is God's act, wherein we are entirely passive; but our becoming 'disciples of Christ' is a voluntary and conscious act of ours, whereby we freely surrender to Christ's lordship and submit to his sceptre. It is by the latter that we obtain evidence of the former. None will yield to the flesh-repellent terms of Christian 'discipleship' save those in whom a Divine work of grace has been wrought, but when that miracle *has* occurred conversion is as certain to follow as a cause will produce its effects. One made a new creature by the Divine miracle of the new birth desires and gladly endeavours to meet the holy requirements of Christ.

Here, then, is the root of spiritual growth: the communication to the soul of spiritual life. Here is what makes possible Christian progress: a person's becoming a Christian, first by the Spirit's anointing and then by his own choice. This twofold signification of the term 'Christian' is the principal key which opens to us the subject of Christian progress or spiritual growth, for it ever needs to be contemplated from both the Divine and human sides. It requires to be viewed both from the angle of God's operations and from that of the discharge of our responsibilities. The twofold meaning of the title 'Christian' must also be borne in mind under the present aspect of our subject, for on the one hand progress is neither necessary nor possible, while in another very real sense it is both desirable and requisite. God's 'anointing' is not susceptible of improvement, being perfect; but our 'discipleship' is to become more intelligent and productive of good works. Much confusion has resulted from ignoring this distinction, and we shall devote the first half of this chapter to the negative side, pointing out those respects in which progress or growth *does not* obtain.

1. Christian progress does not signify advancing in God's favour.

The believer's growth in grace does not further him one iota in God's esteem. How could it, since God is the Giver of his faith and the one who has 'wrought all our works in us' (Isaiah 26:12)! God's favourable regard of his people originated not in anything whatever in them, either actual or foreseen. God's grace is absolutely free, being the spontaneous exercise of his own mere good pleasure. The cause of its exercise lies wholly within himself. The *purposing* grace of God is that good will which he had unto his people from all eternity: 'Who hath saved us and called us with an holy calling, not according to our works, but according to his own purpose and grace which was given us in Christ Jesus before the world began' (2 Timothy 1:9). And the *dispensing* grace of God is but the execution of his purpose, ministering to his people: thus we read 'God *giveth* more grace', yea, that 'he giveth more grace'

(James 4:6). It is entirely gratuitous, sovereignly bestowed, without any inducement being found in its object.

Furthermore, everything God does for and bestows on his people is *for Christ's sake*. It is in nowise a question of their deserts, but of Christ's deserts or what he merited for them. As Christ is the only way by which we can approach the Father, so he is the sole channel through which God's grace flows unto us. Hence we read of the 'grace of God, and the gift of grace (namely, justifying righteousness) by one man, Jesus Christ' (Romans 5:15); and again, 'the grace of God which is given you by Jesus Christ' (1 Corinthians 1:4). The love of God toward us is in 'Christ Jesus our Lord' (Romans 8:39). He forgives us 'for Christ's sake' (Ephesians 4:32). He supplies all our need 'according to his riches in glory by Christ Jesus' (Philippians 4:19). He brings us to heaven in answer to Christ's prayer (John 17:24). Yet though Christ merits everything for us, the original cause was the sovereign grace of God.

> Although the merits of Christ are the (procuring) cause of our salvation, yet they are not the cause of our being ordained to salvation. They are the cause of purchasing all things decreed unto us, but they are not the cause which first moved God to decree these things unto us (Thomas Goodwin).

The Christian is not accepted because of his 'graces', for the very graces (as their name connotes) are bestowed upon him by Divine bounty, and are not attained by any efforts of his. And so far from these graces being the reason why God accepts him, they are the *fruits* of his being 'chosen in Christ before the foundation of the world' and, decretively, 'blessed with all spiritual blessings in the heavenlies in Christ'

(Ephesians 1:3, 4). Settle it then in your own mind once for all, my reader, that growth in grace does not signify growing in the favour of God. This is essentially a Popish delusion, and though creature-flattering it is a horribly Christ-dishonouring one. Since God's elect are 'accepted in the beloved' (Ephesians 1:6), it is impossible that any subsequent change wrought in or attained by them could render them more excellent in his esteem or advance them in his love. When the Father announced concerning the incarnate Word, 'This is my beloved Son (not 'with whom' but) in whom I am well pleased', he was expressing his delight in the whole election of grace, for he was speaking of Christ in his federal character, as the last Adam, as head of his mystical body.

The Christian can neither increase nor decrease in the favour of God, nor can anything he does or fails to do alter or affect to the slightest degree his perfect standing in Christ. Yet let it not be inferred from this that his conduct is of little importance or that God's dealings with him have no relation to his daily walk. While avoiding the Romish conceit of human merits, we must be on our guard against Antinomian licentiousness. As the moral Governor of this world God takes note of our conduct, and in a variety of ways makes manifest his approbation or disapprobation: 'No good thing will he withhold from them that walk uprightly' (Psalm 84:11), yet to his own people God says, 'Your sins have withholden good things from you' (Jeremiah 5:25). So, too, as the Father he maintains discipline in his family, and when his children are refractory he uses the rod (Psalm 89:3-33). Special manifestations of Divine love are granted to the obedient (John 14:21, 23), but are withheld from the disobedient and the careless.

2. Christian progress does not denote that the work of regeneration was incomplete.

Great care needs to be taken in stating this truth of spiritual growth lest we repudiate the perfection of the new birth. When a normal child is born into this world naturally the babe is an entire entity, complete in all its parts, possessing a full set of bodily members and mental faculties. As the child grows there is a strengthening of its body and mind, a development of its members and an expansion of its faculties, with a fuller use of the one and a clearer manifestation of the other; yet no new member or additional faculty is or can be added to him. It is precisely so spiritually. The spiritual life or nature received at the new birth contains within itself all the 'senses' (Hebrews 5:14) and graces, and though these may be nourished and strengthened, and increased by exercise yet not by addition, no, not in heaven itself. 'I know that whatsoever God doeth it shall be forever: nothing can be put to it nor anything taken from it' (Ecclesiastes 3:14). The 'babe' in Christ is just as truly and completely a child of God as the most matured 'father' in Christ.

Regeneration is a more radical and revolutionising change than glorification. The one is a passing from death unto life, the other an entrance into the fullness of life. The one is a bringing into existence of 'the new man which after God is created in righteousness and true holiness' (Ephesians 4:22), the other is a reaching unto the full stature of the new man. The one is a translation into the kingdom of God's dear Son (Colossians 1:13), the other an induction into the higher privileges of that kingdom. The one is the begetting of us unto a living hope (1 Peter 1:3), the other is a realisation of that hope. At regeneration the soul is made a 'new creature' in

Christ, so that 'old things are passed away, behold, all things are become new' (2 Corinthians 5:17). The regenerate soul is a partaker of every grace of the Spirit so that he is 'complete in Christ' (Colossians 2:10), and no growth on earth or glorification in heaven can make him more than complete.

3. Christian progress does not procure a title for heaven. The perfect and indefeasible title of every believer is in the merits of Christ. His vicarious fulfilling of the law, whereby he magnified and made it honourable, secured for all in whose stead he acted the full reward of the law. It is on the all-sufficient ground of Christ's perfect obedience being reckoned to his account that the believer is justified by God and assured that he shall 'reign in life' (Romans 5:17). If he had lived on earth another hundred years and served God perfectly it would add nothing to his title. Heaven is the 'purchased possession' (Ephesians 1:14), purchased for his people by the whole redemptive work of Christ. His precious blood gives every believing sinner the legal right to 'enter the holiest' (Hebrews 10:19). Our title to glory is found alone in Christ. Of the redeemed now in heaven it is said, they have 'washed their robes and made them white in the blood of the Lamb: *therefore* are they before the throne of God and serve him day and night in his temple' (Revelation 7:14, 15).

It has not been sufficiently realised that God's pronouncement of justification is very much more than a mere sense of acquittal or non-condemnation. It includes as well the positive *imputation* of righteousness. As James Hervey so beautifully illustrated it: 'When yonder orb makes his first appearance in the east, what effects are produced? Not only are the shades of night dispersed, but the light of day is diffused. Thus it is when the Author of salvation is manifested to the soul: he brings at once pardon *and acceptance*'. Not only are our 'filthy rags' removed, but the 'best robe' is put upon us (Luke 15:22) and no efforts or attainments of ours can add anything to such a Divine adornment. Christ not only delivered us from death, but purchased life for us; he not only put away our sins but merited an inheritance for us. The most mature and advanced Christian has nought to plead before God for his acceptance than the righteousness of Christ: *that*, nothing but that, and nothing added to it, as his perfect title to Glory.

4. Christian progress does not make us meet for heaven. Many of those who are more or less clear on the three points considered above are far from being so upon this one, and therefore we must enter into it at greater length. Thousands have been taught to believe that when a person has been justified by God and tasted the blessedness of 'the man whose transgression is forgiven, whose sin is covered' that much still remains to be done for the soul before it is ready for the celestial courts. A widespread impression prevails that after his justification the believer must undergo the refining process of sanctification, and that for this he must be left for a time amid the trials and conflicts of a hostile world; yea, so strongly held is this view that some are likely to take exception to what follows. Nevertheless, such a theory repudiates the fact that it is the new-creative work of the Spirit which not only capacitates the soul to take in and enjoy spiritual things now (John 3:3, 5), but also fits it experimentally for the eternal fruition of God.

One had thought that those labouring under the mistake

mentioned above would be corrected by their own experience and by what they observed in their fellow Christians. They frankly acknowledge that their own progress is most unsatisfactory to them, and they have no means of knowing when the process is to be successfully completed. They see their fellow Christians cut off apparently in very varied stages of this process. If it be said that this process is completed only at death, then we would point out that even on their death-beds the most eminent and mature saints have testified to being most humiliated over their attainments and thoroughly dissatisfied with themselves. Their final triumph was not what grace had made them to be in themselves, but what Christ was made to be unto them. If such a view as the above were true, how could any believer cherish a desire to depart and be with Christ (Philippians 1:23) while the very fact that he was still in the body would be proof (according to this idea) that the process was not yet complete to fit him for his presence!

But, it may be asked, is there not such a thing as 'progressive sanctification'? We answer, it all depends on what is signified by that expression. In our judgment it is one which needs to be carefully and precisely defined, otherwise God is likely to be grossly dishonoured and his people seriously injured by being brought into bondage by a most inadequate and defective view of sanctification as a whole. There are several essential and fundamental respects in which sanctification is *not* 'progressive', wherein it admits of no degrees and is incapable of augmentation, and those aspects of sanctification need to be plainly stated and clearly apprehended *before* the subordinate aspect is considered. First, every believer was *decretively* sanctified by God the Father before the foundation of the world (Jude 1). Second, he was *meritoriously* sanctified by God the Son in the redemptive work which he performed in the stead of and on the behalf of his people, so that it is written 'by one offering he hath *perfected forever* them that are sanctified' (Hebrews 10:14). Third, he was *vitally* sanctified by God the Spirit when he quickened him into newness of life, united him to Christ, and made his body his temple.

If by 'progressive sanctification' be meant a clearer understanding and fuller apprehension of what God has made Christ to be unto the believer and of his perfect standing and state in him; if by it be meant the believer living more and more in the enjoyment and power of that, with the corresponding influence and effect it will have upon his character and conduct; if by it be meant a growth of faith and an increase of its fruits, manifested in a holy walk; then we have no objection to the term. But if by 'progressive sanctification' be intended a rendering of the believer more acceptable unto God, or a making of him more fit for the heavenly Jerusalem, then we have no hesitation in rejecting it as a serious error. Not only can there be no increase in the purity and acceptableness of the believer's sanctity before God, but there can be no addition to that holiness of which he became the possessor at the new birth, for the new nature he then received is essentially and impeccably holy.

'The babe in Christ, dying as such, is as capable of as high communion with God as Paul in the state of glory' (S E Pierce).

Instead of striving after and praying that God would make us more fit for heaven, how much better to join with the apostle in 'giving thanks unto the Father who *hath made us meet* to be partakers of the inheritance of the saints in light'

(Colossians 1:12), and then seek to walk suitably unto such a privilege and dignity! *That* is for the saints to '*possess* their possessions' (Obadiah 17); the other is to be robbed of them by a thinly-disguised Romanism. Before pointing out in what the Christian's meetness for heaven consists, let us note that heaven is here termed an 'inheritance'. Now an inheritance is not something we acquire by self-denial and mortification, nor purchase by our own labours or good works; rather it is that to which we lawfully succeed in virtue of our relationship to another. Primarily, it is that to which a child succeeds in virtue to his relationship to his father, or as the son of a king inherits the crown. In this case, the inheritance is ours in virtue of our being *sons of God*.

Peter declares that the Father hath '*begotten* us unto a living hope... *to* an inheritance incorruptible and undefiled and that fadeth not away' (1 Peter 1:4). Paul also speaks of the Holy Ghost witnessing with our spirit that we are the children of God, and then points out: 'and if *children*, then *heirs*; heirs of God and joint-heirs with Christ' (Romans 8:16, 17). If we inquire more distinctly, what is this 'inheritance' of the children of God? Colossians 1:13 tells us that it is the kingdom of God's dear Son. Those who are joint-heirs with Christ must share his kingdom. Already he has made us 'kings and priests unto God' (Revelation 1:5), and the inheritance of kings is a crown, a throne, a kingdom. The blessedness which lies before the redeemed is not merely to be subjects of the King of kings, but to sit with him on his throne, to reign with him for ever (Romans 5:17; Revelation 22:4). Such is the wondrous dignity of our inheritance: as to its *extent*, we are joint-heirs with him whom God 'hath appointed heir of all things' (Hebrews 1:2). Our destiny is bound up with his. O that the faith of Christians would rise above their 'feelings', 'conflicts', and 'experiences', and possess their possessions.

The Christian's title to the inheritance is the righteousness of Christ imputed to him; in what, then, consists his 'meetness'? First, since it be meetness for the inheritance, they must be *children of God*, and this they are made at the moment of regeneration. Second, since it is the 'inheritance of saints', they must be *saints*, and this too they are the moment they believe in Christ, for they are then sanctified by that very blood in which they have forgiveness of sins (Hebrews 13:12). Third, since it is an inheritance 'in light', they must be made *children of light*, and this also they become when God called them 'out of darkness into his marvellous light' (1 Peter 2:9). Nor is that characteristic only of certain specially favoured saints; 'ye are *all* the children of light' (1 Thessalonians 5:5). Fourth, since the inheritance consists of an everlasting kingdom, in order to enjoy it we must have *eternal life*; and that too every Christian possesses: 'he that believeth on the Son of God hath everlasting life' (John 3:36).

'For ye are all the children of God by faith in Christ Jesus' (Galatians 3:26). Are they children in name but not in nature? What a question! It might as well be supposed they have a title to an inheritance and yet be without meetness for it, which would be saying that our sonship was a fiction and not a reality. Very different is the teaching of God's Word: it declares that we become his children by being born again (John 1:13). And regeneration does not consist in the gradual improvement or purification of the old nature, but the creation of a new one. Nor is becoming children of God a lengthy process at all, but an instantaneous thing. The all-mighty agent of it is the Holy Spirit, and obviously that which is born of *him* needs no improving or perfecting. The 'new man' is itself 'created in righteousness and true holiness' (Ephesians 4:22) and certainly *it* cannot stand in need of a 'progressive' work to be wrought in him! True, the old nature opposes all the aspirations and activities of this new nature, and therefore as long as the believer remains in the flesh he is called upon 'through the Spirit to mortify the deeds of the body', yet in spite of the painful and weary conflict, the new nature remains uncontaminated by the vileness in the midst of which he dwells.

That which qualifies the Christian or makes him meet for heaven is the spiritual life which he received at regeneration, for that is the life or nature of God (John 3:5; 2 Peter 1:4). That new life or nature fits the Christian for communion with God, for the presence of God - the same day the dying thief received it, he was with Christ in Paradise! It is true that while we are left here its *manifestation* is obscured, like the sunbeam shining through opaque glass. Yet the sunbeam itself is not dim, though it appears so because of the unsuitable medium through which it passes; but let that opaque glass be removed and it will at once appear in its beauty. So it is with the spiritual life of the Christian: there is no defeat whatever in the life itself but its manifestation is sadly obscured by a mortal body; all that is necessary for the appearing of its perfections is deliverance from the corrupt medium through which it now acts. The life of God in the soul renders a person meet for glory: no attainment of ours, no growth in grace we experience, can *fit* us for heaven any more than it can *entitle* us to it.

If the regeneration of Christians be complete, if their effectual sanctification be effected, if they are already fitted for heaven, then why does God still leave them here on earth? Why not take them to his own immediate presence as soon as they be born again?

Our first answer is, there is no 'if' about it. Scripture distinctly and expressly affirms that even now believers are 'complete in Christ' (Colossians 2:10), that he has 'perfected forever them that are sanctified' (Hebrews 10:14), that they are 'made meet for the inheritance of the saints in light' (Colossians 1:12), and more than 'complete', 'perfect' and 'meet' none will ever be. As to why God - generally, though not always - leaves the babe in Christ in this world for a longer or shorter period: even if no satisfactory reason could be suggested, that would not invalidate to the slightest degree what has been demonstrated, for when any truth is clearly established a hundred objections cannot set it aside. However, while we do not pretend to fathom the mind of God, the following consequences are more or less obvious.

By leaving his people here for a season opportunity is given for:

1. God to manifest his keeping power: not only in a hostile world, but sin still indwelling believers.

2. To demonstrate the sufficiency of his grace: supporting them in their weakness.

3. To maintain a witness for himself in a scene which lieth in the Wicked One.

4. To exhibit his faithfulness in supplying all their need in the wilderness before they reach Canaan.

5. To display his manifold wisdom unto angels (1 Corinthians 4:9; Ephesians 3:10).

6. To act as 'salt' in preserving the race from moral suicide: by the purifying and restraining influence they exert.

7. To make evident the reality of their faith: trusting him in sharpest trials and darkest dispensations.

8. To give them an occasion to glorify him in the place where they dishonoured him.

9. To preach the gospel to those of his elect yet in unbelief.

10. To afford proof that they will serve him amid the most disadvantageous circumstances.

11. To deepen their appreciation of what he has prepared for them.

12. To have fellowship with Christ who endured the cross before he was crowned with glory and honour.

Before showing why Christian progress is necessary let us remind the reader once more of the double significance of the term 'Christian', namely, 'an anointed one' and 'a disciple of Christ', and how this supplies the principal key to the subject before us, intimating its *twofoldness*. His 'anointing' with the Spirit of God is an act of God wherein he is entirely passive, but his becoming a 'disciple of Christ' is a voluntary act of his own, wherein he surrenders to Christ's Lordship and resolves to be ruled by his sceptre. Only as this is duly borne in mind shall we be preserved from error on either side as we pass from one aspect of our theme to another. As the double meaning of the name 'Christian' points to both the Divine operations and human activity, so in the Christian's progress we must keep before us the exercise of God's sovereignty and the discharge of our responsibility. Thus from one angle growth is neither necessary nor possible; from another it is both desirable and requisite. It is from this second angle we are now going to view the Christian, setting forth his obligations therein.

Let us illustrate what has been said above on the twofoldness of this truth by a few simple comments on a well-known verse:

'So teach us to number our days that we may apply our hearts
unto wisdom' (Psalm 90:12). First, this implies that in our
fallen condition we are wayward at heart, prone to follow a
course of folly; and such is our present state by nature.
Second, it implies that the Lord's people have had a discovery
made to them of their woeful case, and are conscious of their
sinful inability to correct the same; which is the experience of
all the regenerate. Third, it signifies an owning of this
humiliating truth, a crying to God for enablement. They beg
to be '*so* taught', as to be actually empowered. In other words,
it is a prayer for enabling grace. Fourth, it expresses the end
in view: 'that *we* may apply our hearts unto wisdom' - perform
our duty, discharge our obligations, conduct ourselves as
'Wisdom's children.' Grace is to be improved, turned to good
account, traded with.

We all know what is meant by a person's 'applying his
mind' to his studies, namely, that he gathers his wandering
thoughts, focuses his attention on the subject before him,
concentrates thereon. Equally evident is a person's 'applying
his *hand*' to a piece of manual labour, namely, that he get
down to business, set himself to the work before him, earnestly endeavour to make a good job of it. In either case there
is an implication: in the former, that he has been given a sound
mind, in the latter that he possesses a healthy body. And in
connection with both cases it is universally acknowledged
that the one *ought* to so employ his mind and the other his
bodily strength. Equally obvious should be the meaning of
and the obligation to 'apply our *hearts* unto wisdom': that is,
diligently, fervently, earnestly make wisdom our quest and
walk in her ways. Since God has given a 'new heart' at
regeneration, it is to be thus employed. If he has quickened us

into newness of life then we ought to grow in grace. If he has made us new creatures in Christ we are to progress as Christians.

Because this will be read by such widely-different classes of readers and we are anxious to help all, we must consider here an objection, for the removal of which we quote the renowned John Owen.

It will be said that if not only the beginning of grace, sanctification, and holiness be *from God*, but the carrying of it on and the increase of it also be from him, and not only so in general, but that all the actings of grace, and every act of it, be an immediate effect of the Holy Spirit, then what need is there that we should take any pains in this thing ourselves, or use our own endeavours to grow in grace and holiness as we are commanded? If God worketh all himself in us, and without his effectual operation in us we can do nothing, there is no place left for our diligence, duty, or obedience.

Answer: (1) This objection we must expect to meet withal at every turn. Men will not believe there is a consistency between God's effectual grace and our diligent obedience; that is, they will not *believe* what is plainly, clearly, distinctly, revealed in the Scripture, and which is suited unto the experience of all that truly believe, because they cannot, it may be, comprehend it within the compass of carnal reason.

(2) Let the apostle answer this objection for this once: 'his Divine power has given unto us all things that pertain unto life and godliness, through the knowledge of him that hath called us to glory and virtue; whereby are given unto us exceeding great and precious promises that by these we might be partakers of the Divine nature, having escaped the corruption that is in the world through lust' (2 Peter 1:3, 4). If all things that pertain unto life and godliness, among which doubtless is the preservation and increase of grace, be given unto us by the power of God; if from him we receive that Divine nature, by virtue whereof our corruptions are subdued, then I pray what need is there of any endeavours of our own? The whole work of sanctification is wrought in us, it

seems, and that by the power of God: we, therefore, may let it
alone and leave it unto him whose it is, whilst we are negligent,
secure and at ease. Nay, says the apostle, this is not *the use* which
the grace of God is to be put unto. The consideration of it is, or
ought to be, the principal motive and encouragement unto all
diligence for the increase of holiness in us. For so he adds
immediately: 'But also for this cause' (Greek) or because of the
gracious operations of the Divine power in us; 'giving all diligence, add to your faith virtue', etc. (v 5).

These objectors and this apostle were very diversely minded
in these matters: what they make an insuperable discouragement
unto diligence in obedience, that he makes the greatest motive and
encouragement thereunto.

(3) I say, from this consideration it will unavoidably follow
that we ought continually to wait and depend on God for supplies
of his Spirit and grace without which we can do nothing; that God
is more the Author by his grace of the good we do than we are
ourselves (not I, but the grace of God that was with me); that we
ought to be careful that by our negligences and sins we provoke
not the Holy Spirit to withhold his aids, and assistances, and so to
leave us to ourselves, in which condition we can do nothing that
is spiritually good; these things, I say, will unavoidably follow on
the doctrine before declared; and if any one be offended at them
it is not in our power to render them relief.

Coming now more directly to the *needs-be* for spiritual
growth or Christian progress. This is not optional but obliga-
tory, for we are expressly bidden to 'Grow in grace and in the
knowledge of our Lord and Saviour Jesus Christ' (2 Peter
3:18) - grow from infancy to the vigour of youth, and from the
zeal of youth to the wisdom of maturity. And again, to be
'building up yourselves in your most holy faith' (Jude 21). It
is not sufficient to be grounded and established in the faith, for
we must grow more and more therein. At conversion we take
upon us the 'yoke' of Christ, and then his word is 'learn of

me', which is to be a lifelong experience. In becoming Christ's disciples we do but enter his school: not to remain in the kindergarten but to progress under his tuition. 'A wise man will hear and increase learning' (Proverbs 1:5), and seek to make good use of that learning. The believer has not yet reached heaven: he is on the way, journeying thither, fleeing from the city of destruction. That is why the Christian life is so often likened unto a *race*, and the believer unto a runner: 'forgetting those things which are behind and reaching forth unto those things which are before, I press toward the mark for the prize' (Philippians 3:13, 14).

1. Only thus is the triune God glorified.

This is so obvious that it really needs no arguing. It brings no glory to God that his children should be dwarfs. As sunshine and rain are sent for the nourishment and fructification of vegetation so the means of grace are provided that we may increase in our spiritual stature. 'As newborn babes desire the sincere milk of the Word that ye may grow thereby' (1 Peter 2:2) - not only in the intellectual knowledge of it, but in a practical conformity thereunto. This should be our chief concern and be made our principal business: to become better acquainted with God, to have the heart more occupied with, and affected by his perfections, to seek after a fuller knowledge of his will, to regulate our conduct thereby, and thus 'show forth the praises of him who hath called us out of darkness into his marvellous light' (1 Peter 2:9). The more we evidence our sonship, the more we conduct ourselves as becometh the children of God before a perverse generation, the more do we honour him who has set his love upon us.

That our spiritual growth and progress *is* glorifying unto

God appears plainly from the prayers of the apostles, for none were more concerned about his glory than they, and nothing occupied so prominent a place in their intercession as this. One or two quotations here must suffice. For the Ephesians Paul prayed, 'that ye might be filled with all the fullness of God' (3:19). For the Philippians, 'that your love may abound yet more and more, in knowledge and in all judgment... being filled with the fruits of righteousness' (1:9-11). For the Colossians, 'that ye might walk worthy of the Lord unto all pleasing, being fruitful in every good work and increasing in the knowledge of God' (1:10, 11). From which we learn that it is our privilege and duty to obtain more spiritual views of the Divine perfections, begetting in us an increasing holy delight in him, making our walk more acceptable. There should be a growing acquaintance with the excellency of Christ, advancing in our love of him, and the more lively exercises of our graces.

2. Only thus do we give proof of our regeneration.
'Herein is my Father glorified, that ye bear much fruit: so shall ye be my disciples' (John 15:8). That does not mean we become the disciples of Christ as a result of our fruitfulness, but that we make manifest we *are* his by our fruitbearing. They who bear no fruit have no vital union with Christ, and like the barren fig-tree, are under his curse. Very solemn is this, and by such a criterion each of us should measure himself. That which is brought forth by the Christian is not to be restricted unto what, in many circles, is called 'service' or 'personal work', but has reference to that which issues from the exercise of all the spiritual graces. Thus: 'Love your enemies, bless them that curse you, do good to them that hate

you and pray for them which despitefully use you and persecute you; that ye may be the children of your Father which is in heaven' (Matthew 5:44, 45), that is, that you may *make it evident* to yourself and fellows that you have been made 'partaker of the Divine nature'.

'Now the works of the flesh are manifest, which are these,' etc., 'but the fruit of the Spirit is love, joy, peace, longsuffering, gentleness, goodness, faith, meekness, temperance' (Galatians 5:19, 22, 23). The reference is not directly to what the Holy Spirit produces, but rather to that which is born of the 'spirit' or new nature of which he is the Author (John 3:6). This is evident from its being set over against the 'works of the flesh' or old nature. It is by means of this 'fruit', these lovely graces, that the regenerate make manifest the presence of a supernatural principle within them. The more such 'fruit' abounds, the clearer our evidence that we have been born again. The total absence of such fruit would prove our profession to have been an empty one. It has often been pointed out by others that what issues from the flesh is designated 'works', for a machine can produce such; but that which the 'spirit' yields is *living* 'fruit' in contrast from 'dead works' (Hebrews 6:1; 9:14). This fruit-bearing is necessary in order to evidence the new birth.

3. Only thus do we certify that we have been made partakers of an effectual call and are among the chosen of God.
'Brethren, give diligence to make your calling and election sure' (2 Peter 1:10) is the Divine exhortation - one which has puzzled many. Yet it should not: it is not to secure it Godward (which is impossible), but to make it more certain to yourselves and your brethren. And how is this to be accomplished?

Why, by acquiring a clearer and fuller evidence of the same: by spiritual growth, for growth is proof that life is present. This interpretation is definitely established by the context. After enumerating the bestowments of Divine grace (vv 3, 4) the apostle says, now here is your responsibility: 'And besides this, giving all diligence, add to your faith (by bringing it into exercise) virtue; and to virtue knowledge; and to knowledge temperance; and to temperance patience; and to patience godliness; and to godliness brotherly kindness; and to brotherly kindness love' (vv 5-7). Faith itself is ever to be operative, but according to different occasions and in their seasons let each of your graces be exercised, and in proportion as they are, the life of holiness is furthered in the soul and there is a proportionate spiritual growth (cf. Colossians 3:12, 13).

4. Only thus do we adorn the doctrine we profess.
The truth we claim to have received into our hearts is 'the doctrine which is according to godliness' (1 Timothy 6:3), and therefore the more our daily lives be conformed thereto the clearer proof do we give that our character and conduct is regulated by *heavenly* principles. It is by our fruits we are known (Matthew 7:16), for 'every good tree bringeth forth good fruit'. Thus, it is only by our being 'fruitful in every good work' (Colossians 1:10) that we make it manifest that we are the 'trees of the Lord' (Psalm 104:16). 'Now are ye light in the Lord, *walk* as children of light' (Ephesians 5:8). It is not the character of our walk which qualifies us to become the children of light, but which demonstrates that we are such. Because we are children of him who is light (1 John 1:5) we must shun the darkness. If we have been 'sanctified in Christ Jesus' (1 Corinthians 1:2) then only that should proceed from

us which 'becometh saints' (Ephesians 5:3). The more we progress in godliness the more we adorn our profession.

5. Only thus do we experience more genuine assurance.

Peace becomes more stable and joy abounds in proportion as we grow in grace and in the knowledge of our Lord and Saviour Jesus Christ, and become more conformed practically to his holy image. It is because so many become slack in using the means of grace and are so little exercised about growing up into Christ 'in all things' (Ephesians 4:16) that doubts and fears possess their hearts. If they do not 'give all diligence to add to their faith' (2 Peter 1:5) by cultivating their several graces, they must not be surprised if they are far from being 'sure' of their Divine calling and election. It is 'the diligent soul', and not the dilatory, who 'shall be made fat' (Proverbs 13:4).

It is the one who makes conscience of obedience and keeps Christ's commandments who is favoured with love-tokens from him (John 14:21). There is an inseparable connection between our being 'led (forward) by the Spirit of God' - which intimates our voluntary concurrence - and his 'bearing witness with our spirit' (Romans 8:14, 16).

6. Only thus are we preserved from grievous backsliding.

In view of much that has been said above this should be quite obvious. The very term 'backsliding' denotes failure to make progress and go forward. Peter's denial of Christ in the high priest's palace was preceded by his following him 'afar off' (Matthew 26:58), and that has been recorded for our learning and warning. The same principle is illustrated again in connection with the awful fall of David. Though it was 'at the time when kings go forth to battle' he was selfishly and lazily taking his ease, and while so lax succumbed to temptation (1 Samuel 11:1, 2). Unless we 'follow on to know the Lord' and learn to make use of the armour which he has provided, we shall easily be overcome by the enemy. Only as our hearts are kept healthy and our affections set upon things above shall we be impervious to the attractions of this world. We cannot be stationary: if we do not grow, we shall decline.

7. Only thus shall we preserve the cause of Christ from reproach.
The backsliding of his people makes his enemies to blaspheme - how many have taken occasion to do so from the sad case of David! When the world sees us halting, it is gratified, being bolstered up in their idea that godliness is but a pose, a sham. Because of this, among other reasons, Christians are bidden to 'be blameless and harmless, the sons of God, without rebuke in the midst of a crooked and perverse nation, among whom shine ye as lights in the world' (Philippians 2:15). If we go backward instead of forward - and we *must* do one or the other - then we greatly dishonour the name of Christ and fill his foes with unholy glee. Rather is it 'the will of God that with well-doing we put to silence the ignorance of foolish men' (1 Peter 2:15). The longer they remain in this world, the more apparent should be the contrast between the children of light and those who are the subjects of the Prince of darkness. Very necessary then, from many considerations, is our growth in grace.

CHAPTER 5

The Scriptures and Prayer

A prayerless Christian is a contradiction in terms. Just as a still-born child is a dead one, so a professing believer who does not pray is devoid of spiritual life. Prayer is the breath of the new nature in the saint, as the Word of God is its food. When the Lord would assure the Damascus disciple, Ananias, that Saul of Tarsus had been truly converted, he told him, 'Behold, he prayeth' (Acts 9:11). On many occasions had that self-righteous Pharisee bowed his knees before God and gone through his 'devotions', but this was the first time he had ever really *prayed*. This important distinction needs emphasising in this day of powerless forms (2 Timothy 3:5). They who content themselves with formal addresses to God know him not; for 'the spirit of grace *and* supplications' (Zechariah 12:10) are never separated. God has no dumb children in his regenerated family: 'Shall not God avenge his own elect, which cry day and night unto him?' (Luke 18:7). Yes, 'cry' unto him, not merely 'say' their prayers.

But will the reader be surprised when the writer declares it is his deepening conviction that, probably, the Lord's own people sin more in their efforts to pray than in connection with any other thing they engage in? What hypocrisy there is, where there should be reality! What presumptuous demandings, where there should be submissiveness! What formality, where there should be brokenness of heart! How little we really *feel*

the sins we confess, and what little *sense* of deep need for the
mercies we seek! And even where God grants a measure of
deliverance from these awful sins, how much coldness of
heart, how much unbelief, how much self-will and self-
pleasing have we to bewail! Those who have no conscience
upon these things are strangers to the spirit of holiness.

Now the Word of God should be our directory in prayer.
Alas, how often we have made our own fleshly inclinations
the rule of our asking. The Holy Scriptures have been given
to us 'that the man of God may be perfect, thoroughly
furnished unto all good works' (2 Timothy 3:17). Since we are
required to 'pray in the Spirit' (Jude 20), it follows that our
prayers ought to be according to the Scriptures, seeing that he
is their Author throughout. It equally follows that according
to the measure in which the Word of Christ dwells in us
'richly' (Colossians 3:16) or sparsely, the more or the less will
our petitions be in harmony with the mind of the Spirit, for
'out of the abundance of the heart the mouth speaketh'
(Matthew 12:34). In proportion as we hide the Word in our
hearts, and it cleanses, moulds and regulates our inner man,
will our prayers be acceptable in God's sight. Then shall we
be able to say, as David did in another connection, 'Of thine
own have we given thee' (1 Chronicles 29:14).

Thus the purity and power of our prayer-life are another
index by which we may determine the extent to which we are
profiting from our reading and searching of the Scriptures. If
our Bible study is not, under the blessing of the Spirit,
convicting us of the sin of prayerlessness, revealing to us the
place which prayer ought to have in our daily lives, and
actually bringing us to spend more time in the secret place of
the Most High; unless it is teaching us how to pray more

acceptably to God, how to appropriate his promises and plead them before him, how to appropriate his precepts and turn them into petitions, then not only has the time we spend over the Word been to little or no soul enrichment, but the very knowledge that we have acquired of its letter will only add to our condemnation in the day to come. 'Be ye doers of the word, and not hearers only, deceiving your own selves' (James 1:22) applies to its prayer-admonitions as to everything else in it. Let us now point out seven criteria.

1. We are profited from the Scriptures when we are brought to realise *the deep importance of prayer*. It is really to be feared that many present-day readers (and even students) of the Bible have no deep convictions that a definite prayer-life is absolutely essential to a daily walking and communing with God, as it is for deliverance from the power of indwelling sin, the seductions of the world, and the assaults of Satan. If such a conviction really gripped their hearts, would they not spend far more time on their faces before God? It is worse than idle to reply, 'A multitude of duties which have to be performed crowd out prayer, though much against my wishes.' But the fact remains that each of us takes time for anything we deem to be imperative. Who ever lived a busier life than our Saviour? Yet who found more time for prayer? If we truly yearn to be suppliants and intercessors before God and use all the available time we now have, he will so order things for us that we shall have more time.

The lack of positive conviction of the deep importance of prayer is plainly evidenced in the corporate life of professing Christians. God has plainly said, 'My house shall be called the house of prayer' (Matthew 21:13). Note, not 'the house of preaching and singing', but of *prayer*. Yet, in the great majority of even so-called orthodox churches, the ministry of prayer has become a negligible quantity. There are still evangelistic campaigns, and Bible-teaching conferences, but how rarely one hears of two weeks set apart for special prayer! And how much good do these 'Bible conferences' accomplish if the prayer-life of the churches is not strengthened? But when the Spirit of God applies in power to our hearts such words as, 'Watch ye and pray, lest ye enter into temptation' (Mark 14:38), 'In every thing by prayer and supplication with thanksgiving let your requests be made known to God' (Philippians 4:6), 'Continue in prayer, and watch in the same with thanksgiving' (Colossians 4:2), then are we being profited from the Scriptures.

2. We are profited from the Scriptures when we are made to feel that *we know not how to pray*. 'We know not what we should pray for as we ought' (Romans 8:26). How very few professing Christians really believe this! The idea most generally entertained is that people know well enough what they should pray for, only they are careless and wicked, and so fail to pray for what they are fully assured is their duty. But such a conception is at direct variance with this inspired declaration in Romans 8:26. It is to be observed that that flesh-humbling affirmation is made not simply of men in general, but of the saints of God in particular, among which the apostle did not hesitate to include himself: '*We* know not what we should pray for as we ought.' If this be the condition of the regenerate, how much more so of the unregenerate! Yet it is one thing to read and mentally assent to what this verse says, but it is quite another to have an experimental realisation of it, for the heart to be made to feel that what God requires from us he must *himself* work in and through us.

I often say my prayers,
But do I ever pray?
And do the wishes of my heart
Go with the words I say?
I may as well kneel down
And worship gods of stone,
As offer to the living God
A prayer of words alone.

It is many years since the writer was taught these lines by his mother - now 'present with the Lord' - but their searching message still comes home with force to him. The Christian can no more *pray* without the direct enabling of the Holy Spirit than he can create a world. This must be so, for real prayer is a felt need awakened within us by the Spirit, so that we ask God, in the name of Christ, for that which is in accord with his holy will. 'If we ask any thing according to his will, he heareth us' (1 John 5:14). But to ask something which is not according to God's will is not praying, but presuming. True, God's revealed will is made known in his Word, yet not in such a way as a cookery book contains recipes and directions for preparing various dishes. The Scriptures frequently enumerate principles which call for continuous exercise of heart and Divine help to show us their application to different cases and circumstances. Thus we are being profited from the Scriptures when we are taught our deep need of crying 'Lord, *teach* us to pray' (Luke 11:1), and are actually constrained to beg him for the spirit of prayer.

3. We are profited from the Scriptures when we are made conscious *of our need of the Spirit's help*. First, that he may make known to us our real wants. Take, for example, our temporal needs. How often we are in some external strait; things from without press hard upon us, and we long to be

delivered from these trials and difficulties. Surely *here* we 'know' of ourselves *what* to pray for. No, indeed; far from it! The truth is that, despite our natural desire for relief, so ignorant are we, so dull is our discernment, that (even where there is an exercised conscience) we know not what submission unto his pleasure God may require, or how he may sanctify these afflictions to our inward good. Therefore, God calls the petitions of most who seek for relief from external trials 'howlings', and not a crying unto him with the heart (see Hosea 7:14). 'For who knoweth what is good for man in this life?' (Ecclesiastes 6:12). Ah, heavenly wisdom is needed to teach us our temporal 'needs' so as to make them a matter of prayer according to the mind of God.

Perhaps a few words need to be added to what has just been said. Temporal things *may be* scripturally prayed for (Matthew 6:11, etc.), but with this threefold limitation. First, *incidentally* and not primarily, for they are not the things which Christians are principally concerned with (Matthew 6:33). It is heavenly and eternal things (Colossians 3:1) which are to be sought first and foremost, as being of far greater importance and value than temporal things. Second, *subordinately*, as a means to an end. In seeking material things from God it should not be in order that we may be gratified, but as an aid to our pleasing him better. Third, *submissively*, not dictatorially, for that would be the sin of presumption. Moreover, we know not whether any temporal *mercy* would really contribute to our highest good (Psalm 106:18), and therefore we must leave it with God to decide.

We have inward wants as well as outward. Some of these may be discerned in the light of conscience, such as the guilt and defilement of sin, of sins against light and nature and the plain letter of the law. Nevertheless, the knowledge which we have of ourselves by means of the conscience is so dark and confused that, apart from the Spirit, we are in no way able to discover the true fountain of cleansing. The things about which believers do and ought to treat primarily with God in their supplications are the inward frames and spiritual dispositions of their souls. Thus, David was not satisfied with confessing all known transgressions and his original sin (Psalm 51:1-5), nor yet with an acknowledgment that none could understand his errors, whence he desired to be cleansed from 'secret faults' (Psalm 19:12); but he also begged God to undertake the inward searching of his heart to find out what was amiss in him (Psalm 139:23,24), knowing that God principally requires 'truth in the inward parts' (Psalm 51:6). Thus, in view of 1 Corinthians 2:10-12, we should definitely seek the Spirit's aid that we may pray acceptably to God.

4. We are profited from the Scriptures when the Spirit teaches us *the right end in praying*. God has appointed the ordinance of prayer with at least a threefold design. First, that the great triune God might be honoured, for prayer is an act of worship, a paying homage; to the Father as the Giver, in the Son's name, by whom alone we may approach him, by the moving and directing power of the Holy Spirit. Second, to humble our hearts for prayer is ordained to bring us into the place of dependence, to develop within us a sense of our helplessness, by owning that without the Lord we can do nothing, and that we are beggars upon his charity for everything we are and have. But how feebly is this realised (if at all) by any of us until the Spirit takes us in hand, removes pride from us, and gives God his true place in our hearts and thoughts. Third, as a means or way of obtaining for ourselves

the good things for which we ask.

It is greatly to be feared that one of the principal reasons why so many of our prayers remain unanswered is because we have a wrong, an unworthy end in view. Our Saviour said, 'Ask, and it shall be given you' (Matthew 7:7): but James affirms of some, 'Ye ask, and receive not, because ye ask amiss, that ye may consume it upon your lusts' (James 4:3). To pray for anything, and not expressly unto the end which God has designed, is to 'ask amiss', and therefore to no purpose. Whatever confidence we may have in our own wisdom and integrity, if we are left to ourselves our aims will never be suited to the will of God. Unless the Spirit restrains the flesh within us, our own natural and distempered affections intermix themselves in our supplications, and thus are rendered vain. 'Whatsoever ye do, do all to the glory of God' (1 Corinthians 10:31), yet none but the Spirit can enable us to subordinate all our desires unto God's glory.

5. We are profited from the Scriptures when we are taught *how to plead God's promises*. Prayer must be in faith (Romans 10:14), or God will not hear it. Now faith has respect to God's promises (Hebrews 4:1; Romans 4:21); if, therefore, we do not understand what God stands pledged to give, we cannot pray at all. The promises of God contain the matter of prayer and define the measure of it. What God has promised, all that he has promised, and nothing else, we are to pray for. 'Secret things belong unto the LORD our God' (Deuteronomy 29:29), but the declaration of his will and the revelation of his grace belong unto us, and are our rule. There is nothing that we really stand in need of but God has promised to supply it, yet in such a way and under such limitations as will make it good and useful to us. So too there is nothing God has

promised but we stand in need of it, or are some way or other concerned in it as members of the mystical body of Christ. Hence, the better we are acquainted with the Divine promises, and the more we are enabled to understand the goodness, grace and mercy prepared and proposed in them, the better equipped are we for acceptable prayer.

Some of God's promises are general rather than specific; some are conditional, others unconditional; some are fulfilled in this life, others in the world to come. Nor are we able of ourselves to discern which promise is most suited to our particular case and present emergency and need, or to appropriate by faith and rightly plead it before God. Wherefore we are expressly told, 'For what man knoweth the things of a man save the spirit of man which is in him? Even so the things of God knoweth no man, but the Spirit of God. Now we have received, not the spirit of the world but the Spirit which is of God; that we might know the things that are freely given to us of God' (1 Corinthians 2:11, 12). Should someone reply, If so much be required unto acceptable praying, if we cannot supplicate God aright without much less trouble than you indicate, few will continue long in this duty, then we answer that such an objector knows not what it is to pray, nor does he seem willing to learn.

6. We are profited from the Scriptures when we are brought to *complete submission unto God*. As stated above, one of the Divine designs in appointing prayer as an ordinance is that we might be humbled. This is outwardly denoted when we bow the knee before the Lord. Prayer is an acknowledgment of our helplessness, and a looking to him from whom all our help comes. It is an owning of his sufficiency to supply our every need. It is a making known our 'requests' (Philippians 4:6)

unto God; but requests are very different from *demands*. 'The throne of grace is not set up that we may come and there vent our passions before God' (William Gurnall). We are to spread our case before God, but leave it to his superior wisdom to prescribe how it shall be dealt with. There must be no dictating, nor can we 'claim' anything from God, for we are beggars dependent upon his mere mercy. In all our praying we must add, 'Nevertheless, not as I will, but as thou wilt.'

But may not faith plead God's promises and expect an answer? Certainly; but it must be *God's* answer. Paul besought the Lord thrice to remove his thorn in the flesh; instead of doing so, the Lord gave him grace to endure it (2 Corinthians 12). Many of God's promises are promiscuous rather than personal. He has promised his Church pastors, teachers and evangelists, yet many a local company of his saints has languished long without them. Some of God's promises are indefinite and general rather than absolute and universal; as, for example Ephesians 6:2, 3. God has not bound himself to give in kind or specie, to grant the particular thing we ask for, even though we ask in faith. Moreover, he reserves to *himself* the right to determine the fit time and season for bestowing his mercies. 'Seek ye the LORD, all ye meek of the earth... it *may be* ye shall be hid in the day of the LORD's anger' (Zephaniah 2:3). Just because it 'may be' God's will to grant a certain temporal mercy unto me, it is my duty to cast myself upon him and plead for it, yet with entire submission to his good pleasure for the performance of it.

7. We are profited from the Scriptures when prayer becomes *a real and deep joy*. Merely to 'say our prayers' each morning and evening is an irksome task, a duty to be performed which brings a sigh of relief when it is done. But really

to come into the conscious presence of God, to behold the glorious light of his countenance, to commune with him at the mercy seat, is a foretaste of the eternal bliss awaiting us in heaven. The one who is blessed with this experience says with the Psalmist, 'It is good for me to draw near to God' (Psalm 73:28). Yes, good for the heart, for it is quietened; good for faith, for it is strengthened; good for the soul, for it is blessed. It is lack of this soul communion with God which is the root cause of our unanswered prayers: 'Delight thyself also in the LORD; and he *shall* give thee the desires of thine heart' (Psalm 37:4).

What is it which, under the blessing of the Spirit, produces and promotes this joy in prayer?

First, it is the heart's delight in God as the Object of prayer, and particularly the recognition and realisation of God as *our Father*. Thus, when the disciples asked the Lord Jesus to teach them to pray, he said, 'After this manner therefore pray ye: Our Father which art in heaven.' And again, 'God hath sent forth the Spirit of his Son into your hearts, crying, Abba (the Hebrew for 'Father'), Father' (Galatians 4:6), which includes a filial, holy delight in God, such as children have in their parents in their most affectionate addresses to them. So again, in Ephesians 2:18, we are told, for the strengthening of faith and the comfort of our hearts, 'For through him (Christ) we both have access by one Spirit unto *the Father*.' What peace, what assurance, what freedom this gives to the soul: to know we are approaching our Father!

Second, joy in prayer is furthered by the heart's apprehension and the soul's sight of God as on the throne of *grace* - a sight or prospect, not by carnal imagination, but by spiritual illumination, for it is by faith that we 'see him who is invisible'

(Hebrews 11:27); faith being the 'evidence of things not seen' (Hebrews 11:1), making its proper object evident and present unto them that believe. Such a sight of God upon such a 'throne' cannot but thrill the soul. Therefore are we exhorted, 'Let us therefore come boldly unto the throne of grace, that we may obtain mercy, and find grace to help in time of need' (Hebrews 4:16).

Thirdly, and drawn from the last quoted Scripture, freedom and delight in prayer are stimulated by the consciousness that God is, through Jesus Christ, willing and ready to dispense grace and mercy to suppliant sinners. There is no reluctance in him which we have to overcome. He is more ready to give than we are to receive. So he is represented in Isaiah 30:18, 'And therefore will the LORD wait, that he may be gracious unto you.' Yes, he waits to be sought unto; waits for faith to lay hold of his readiness to bless. His ear is ever open to the cries of the righteous. Then 'let us draw near with a true heart in *full assurance of faith*' (Hebrews 10:22); 'in *every thing* by prayer and supplication with thanksgiving let your requests be made known unto God', and we shall find that peace which passes all understanding guarding our hearts and minds through Christ Jesus (Philippians 4:6, 7).

CHAPTER 6

The Ten Commandments

Much confusion prevails today among those who speak of 'the law'. This is a term which needs to be carefully defined. In the New Testament there are three expressions used which require to be definitely distinguished. First, there is 'the law *of God*' (Romans 7:22, 25, etc.). Second, there is 'the law *of Moses*' (John 7:2; Acts 13: 39, 15:5, etc.). Third, there is 'the law *of Christ*' (Galatians 6:2). Now these three expressions are by no means synonymous, and it is not until we learn to distinguish between them, that we can hope to arrive at any clear understanding on the subject of 'the law'.

The 'law of God' expresses the mind of the *Creator*, and is binding upon all rational creatures. It is God's unchanging moral standard for regulating the conduct of all men. In some places the 'law of God' may refer to the whole revealed will of God, but usually it has reference to the Ten Commandments, and it is in this restricted sense we shall here use the term. The law was impressed on man's moral nature from the beginning, and though now fallen, he still shows the work of it written on his heart. This law has never been repealed, and, in the very nature of things, cannot be. For God to abrogate the moral law would be to plunge the whole universe into anarchy. Obedience to the law of God is man's first duty. This is why the first complaint that Jehovah made against Israel after they left Egypt was 'How long refuse ye to keep my

commandments and my laws?' (Exodus 16:2, 27). That is
why the first statutes which God gave to Israel after their
redemption were the Ten Commandments, i.e. the moral law.
That is why in the first discourse of Christ recorded in the New
Testament, he declared, 'Think not that I am come to destroy
the law, or the prophets: I am not come to destroy, but to fulfil'
(Matthew 5:17), and then proceeded to expound and enforce
the moral law. And that is why in the first of the Epistles, the
Holy Spirit has taught us at length the relation of the law to
sinners and saints, in connection with salvation and the subsequent walk of the saved: the word 'law' occurs in Romans no less
than seventy-five times, though, of course, not every reference
is to the law of God. And that is why sinners (Romans 3:19)
and saints (James 2:12) shall be judged by this law.

The *'law of Moses'* is the entire system of legislation,
judicial and ceremonial, which Jehovah gave to Israel during
the time they were in the wilderness. The 'law of Moses', as
such, is binding upon none but Israelites. The 'law of Moses'
has not been repealed, for it will be enforced by Christ during
the Millennium. 'Out of Jerusalem shall go forth the Law, and
the Word of the LORD *from Jerusalem*' (Isaiah 2:3). That the
'law of Moses' *is not* binding on Gentiles is clear from Acts 15.

The *'law of Christ'* is God's moral law in the hands of a
Mediator. It is the law that Christ himself was 'made under'
(Galatians 4:4). It is the law which was 'in his heart' (Psalm
40:8). It is the law which he came to 'fulfil' (Matthew 5:17).
The 'law of God' is now termed 'the law of Christ' as it relates
to Christians. As *creatures* we are under bonds to 'serve the
law of God' (Romans 7:25): as *redeemed sinners* we are
'bondslaves of Christ' (Ephesians 6:6) and as such it is our
bounden duty to 'serve the Lord Christ' (Colossians 3:2b).

The relation between these two appellations, 'the law of God' and 'the law of Christ' is clearly intimated in 1 Corinthians 9:21, where the apostle states that he *was not* 'without law to God' for he *was* 'under the law to Christ'. The meaning of this is very simple. As a human creature, the apostle was still under obligations to obey the moral law of God, his Creator; but as a saved man he now belongs to Christ, the Mediator by redemption. Christ had purchased him, he was his, therefore was under the 'law of Christ'. The 'law of Christ' then, is just the moral law of God now in the hands of the Mediator - cf. Exodus 34:1 and what follows!

Should any one object against our definition of the distinction drawn between God's moral law and 'the law of Moses' we request them to attend closely to what follows. God took special pains to show us the clear line of demarcation which he himself has drawn between the two. The moral law became incorporated in the Mosaic law, yet was it sharply distinguished from it.

In the first place, the Ten Commandments and *they alone* of all the laws which God gave unto Israel, were *promulgated* by the voice of God, amid the most solemn manifestations and tokens of the Divine presence. Second, the Ten Commandments and they alone of all Jehovah's statutes to Israel, were *written directly* by the finger of God, written *upon tables of stone*, and written thus to denote their lasting and imperishable nature. Third, the Ten Commandments were distinguished from all the other laws which had merely a local application to Israel by the fact that *they alone were laid up in the ark*. A tabernacle was prepared by the special direction of God, and within it an ark was placed, in which the two tablets of stone were deposited. The ark, formed of the most durable wood,

was overlaid with gold within and without. Over it was placed
the mercy seat, which became the throne of Jehovah in the
midst of his redeemed people. Not until the tabernacle had
been erected and the law placed in the ark, did Jehovah take
up his abode in Israel's midst. Thus did the Lord signify to
Israel that the moral law was the basis of all his governmental
dealings with them!

It is therefore clear beyond room for doubt that the Ten
Commandments are to be sharply distinguished from the 'law
of Moses'. The 'law of Moses', excepting the Moral Law
incorporated therein, was binding upon none but Israelites or
Gentile proselytes. But the 'law of God' unlike the Mosaic, is
binding upon all men. Once this distinction is perceived,
many minor difficulties are cleared up. For example: someone says, if we are to keep the Sabbath-day holy, as Israel did,
why must we not observe the other 'Sabbaths' - the Sabbatic
year, for instance? The answer is, Because the moral law
alone is binding upon Gentiles and Christians. But why, it
may be asked, does not the death penalty attached to the
desecration of the Sabbath day (Exodus 31:14, etc.) still
obtain? The answer is, Because though *that* was a part of the
Mosaic law, it was not a part of the moral law, i.e. it was not
inscribed on the tables of stone: therefore it concerned none
but Israelites. Let us now consider separately, but briefly,
each of the Ten Commandments.

The *order* of the Commandments is most significant. The
first four concern human responsibility *Godwards*; the last
five our obligations *manwards*: while the fifth suitably bridges
the two, for in a certain sense parents occupy to their children
the place of God. We may also add that the substance of each
commandment is in perfect keeping with its numerical place

in the Decalogue. One stands for *unity* and *supremacy* so in the first commandment the absolute *sovereignty* and pre-eminency of the Creator is insisted upon. Since God is who he is, he will tolerate no competitor or rival: *his* claims upon us are paramount.

The first commandment

If this first commandment received the respect it demands, obedience to the other nine would follow as a matter of course. 'Thou shalt have no other gods before me' means, thou shalt have no other object of worship: thou shalt own no other authority as absolute: thou shalt make me *supreme* in your hearts and lives. How much this first commandment contains! There are other 'gods' besides idols of wood and stone. Money, pleasure, fashion, fame, gluttony, and a score of other things which make self supreme, usurp the rightful place of God in the affections and thoughts of many. It is not without reason that even to the saints the exhortation is given, 'Little children, keep yourselves from idols' (1 John 5:21).

The second commandment

Two is the number of *witness*, and in this second commandment man is forbidden to attempt any visible representation of Deity, whether furnished by the skill of the artist or the sculptor. The first commandment points out the one only object of worship: the second tells us *how* he is to be worshipped - in spirit and in truth, by faith and not by images which appeal to the senses. The design of this commandment is to draw us away from carnal conceptions of God, and to prevent his worship being profaned by superstitious rites. A most fearful threat and a most gracious promise are attached.

Those who break this commandment shall bring down on their children the righteous judgment of God: those who keep it shall cause mercy to be extended to thousands of those who love God. How this shows us the vital and solemn importance of parents teaching their children the unadulterated truth concerning the Being and Character of God!

The third commandment
God requires that the majesty of his holy name be held inviolably sacred by us. His name must be used neither with contempt, irreverently, or needlessly. It is striking to observe that the *first* petition in the prayer the Lord taught his disciples is, 'Hallowed be thy *name*'! The name of God is to be held profoundly sacred. In our ordinary speech and in our religious devotions nothing must enter that in any wise lowers the sublime dignity and the high holiness of that Name. The greatest sobriety and reverence is called for. It needs to be pointed out that the only time the word 'reverend' is found in the Bible is in Psalm 111:9 where we read 'Holy and reverend is *his* name'. How irreverent then for preachers to style *themselves* 'reverend'!

The fourth commandment
There are two things enjoined here: first, that man should work six days of the week. The same rule is plainly enforced in the New Testament: 'And that ye study to be quiet, and to do your own business, and to *work* with *your own* hands, as we *commanded* you' (1 Thessalonians 4:11). 'For even when we were with you this we commanded you, that if any would not *work, neither should he eat*' (2 Thessalonians 3:10)! The second thing commanded is that on the seventh day all work must cease. The Sabbath is to be a day of *rest*. Six days work:

one day for rest. The two must not be separated: work calls for rest: rest for work.

The next thing we would observe is that the Sabbath is *not* here termed 'the seventh day *of the week*'. Nor is it ever so styled in Scripture! So far as the Old Testament is concerned any day which was used for rest, and which was followed by six days of work was a Sabbath! It is not correct then, to say that the 'Sabbath' can *only be* observed on a *Saturday*. There is not a word of Scripture to support such a statement.

In the next place, we emphatically deny that this Sabbath law has *ever been repealed*. Those who teach it has, are guilty of the very thing which the Saviour so pointedly condemns in Matthew 5:19. There are those who allow that it is right and proper for us to keep the other nine Commandments, but they insist that the Sabbath has passed away. We fully believe that this very error was anticipated by Christ in Matthew 5:19: 'Whosoever shall break *one* (not 'any one') of these least commandments, and shall teach men so, he shall be called the least in the kingdom of heaven'. Hebrews 4:9 tells us that Sabbath-keeping *remains*: it has *not* become obsolete.

The Sabbath (like all the other Commandments) was not simply for Israel but for all men. The Lord Jesus distinctly declared 'the Sabbath was made for *man*' (Mark 2:27) and no amount of quibbling can ever make this mean *Jews only*. The Sabbath was made for man: for man to observe and obey; also for man's well-being, because his constitution needed it. One day of rest each week is requisite for man's physical, mental and spiritual good.

But we must not mistake the means for the end. We must not think that the Sabbath is just for the sake of being able to attend meetings. There are some people who think they must spend the whole day at meetings or private devotions. The result is that at nightfall they are tired out and the day has brought them no rest. The number of church services attended ought to be measured by the person's ability to enjoy them and get good from them, *without being wearied*. Attending meetings is not the only way to observe the Sabbath. The Israelites were commanded to *keep it in their dwellings* as well as in holy convocation. The home, that centre of so great influence over the life and character of the people, ought to be made the scene of true Sabbath observance (D L Moody).

The fifth commandment

The word 'honour' means more than obey, though obedience is necessarily included in it. To 'honour' a parent is to give him the place of superiority, to hold him or her in high esteem, to reverence him. The Scriptures abound with illustrations of Divine blessing coming upon those who honoured their parents, and the Divine curse descending on those who honoured them not. The supreme example is that of the Lord Jesus. In Luke 2:52, we read, 'And he went down with them and came to Nazareth, and was *subject unto them*'. On the Cross we see the Saviour honouring his mother by providing a home for her with his beloved disciple John.

It is indeed sad to see the almost universal disregard of this fifth Commandment in our own day. It is one of the most arresting of the many 'signs of the times'. Eighteen hundred years ago it was foretold, 'In the last days perilous times shall come. For men shall be lovers of their own selves, covetous, boasters, proud, blasphemous, disobedient to parents, unthankful, unholy, *without natural affection*' (2 Timothy 3:1, 3). Unquestionably, the *blame* for most of this lies upon the parents, who have so neglected the moral and spiritual training of their children that (in themselves) they are worthy of neither respect nor honour. It is to be noted that the promise attached to the fulfilment of this Commandment as well as the command itself is repeated in the New Testament (see Ephesians 6:1, 3).

The sixth commandment

The simple force of this is, thou shalt not murder. God himself has attached the death-penalty to murder. This comes out plainly in Genesis 9:5, 6. 'And surely your blood of your lives will I require: at the hand of every beast will I require it, and at the hand of man; at the hand of every man's brother will I require the life of man. Whoso sheddeth man's blood, by man shall his blood be shed, for in the image of God made he man.' This statute which God gave to Noah has *never been rescinded*. In Matthew 5:21, 22, we have Christ's exposition of this sixth commandment: he goes deeper than the letter of the words and gives the spirit of them. He shows that murder is not limited to the overt act, but also pertains to the state of mind and the angry passion which prompts the act (cf. 1 John 3:15).

In this sixth Commandment, God emphasises the sacredness of human life and his own sovereignty over it - he alone has the right to say when it shall end. The force of this was taught Israel in connection with the cities of refuge. These provided an asylum from the avenger of blood. But they were not to shelter murderers, but only those who had killed 'unwittingly' (RV). It was only those who had unintentionally taken the life of a fellow-creature who could take refuge therein! And this, be it observed, was not regarded as a light affair: even the man who had taken life 'unawares' was deprived of his liberty until the death of the high priest!

The seventh commandment

This respects the marriage relationship which was instituted
in Eden: 'Therefore shall a man leave his father and his
mother, and shall cleave unto his wife: and they shall be one
flesh' (Genesis 2:24). The marriage-relationship is paramount over every other human obligation. A man is more
responsible to love and care for his wife than he is to remain
in the home of his childhood and take care of his father and
mother. It is the highest and most sacred of human relations.
It is in view of this relationship that the seventh Commandment is given. 'Thou shalt not commit adultery' means, thou
shalt not be unfaithful to the marriage obligations.

Now in Christ's exposition of this Commandment we find
him filling it out and giving us its deeper meaning: 'I say unto
you, That whosoever looketh on a woman to lust after her hath
committed adultery with her already in his heart' (Matthew
5:18). Unfaithfulness is not limited to the overt act, but
reaches to the passions behind the act. In Christ's interpretation of the law of divorce he shows that one thing only can
dissolve the marriage relationship, and that is unfaithfulness
on the part of the husband or the wife. 'I say unto you,
Whosoever shall put away his wife, *except for fornication*,
and shall marry another, committeth adultery and whoso
marrieth her which is put away doth commit adultery' (Matthew 19:9). Fornication is the general term; adultery the
specific: the former includes the latter. 1 Corinthians 7:15
supplies no exception: if one *depart* from the other, except it
be on the ground of *unfaithfulness*, neither is free to marry
again. Separation *is not divorce* in the *scriptural sense*. 'If she
depart, let her remain unmarried' (1 Corinthians 7:11).

The eighth commandment

The design of this Commandment is to inculcate honesty in all our dealings with men. Stealing covers more than pilfering. 'Owe no man anything' (Romans 13:8). 'Providing for honest things, not only in the sight of the Lord, but also in the sight of men' (2 Corinthians 8:21). I may steal from another by fraudulent means, without using any violence. If I borrow a book and fail to return it, that is *theft* - it is keeping what is not my own. How many are guilty here! If I misrepresent an article for sale, the price which I receive over and above its fair market value is *stolen*! The man who obtains money by gambling receives money for which he has done no honest work, and is therefore a thief!

> Parents are woefully lax in their condemnation and punishment of the sin of stealing. The child begins by taking sugar, it may be. The mother makes light of it at first and the child's conscience is violated without any sense of wrong. By and by it is not an easy matter to check the habit, because it grows and multiplies with every new commission (D L Moody).

The ninth commandment

The scope of these words is much wider than is generally supposed. The most flagrant form of this sin is to slander our neighbours - a lie invented and circulated with malicious intentions. Few forms of injury done by one man to another is more despicable than this. But equally reprehensible is tale-bearing where there has been no careful investigation to verify the evil report. False witness may be borne by leaving a false impression upon the minds of people by a mere hint or suggestion. 'Have you heard about Mr so-and-so?' 'No.' 'Ah! Well, the least said the soonest mended.' Again, when one makes an unjust criticism or charge against another in the hearing of a third party, and that third party remains silent, his very silence is a breach of this ninth Commandment. The flattering of another, exaggerated eulogy, is a *false* witness. Rightly has it been said, 'There is no word of the Decalogue more often and more unconsciously broken than this ninth Commandment, and men need perpetually and persistently to pray, Set a watch, O Lord, before my mouth: keep the door of my lips.'

The tenth commandment
This Commandment differs from all the others in that while they prohibit the overt act, this condemns the very desire to act. The word 'covet' means *desire*, and the Commandment forbids us to covet *any thing* that is our neighbour's. Clear proof is this that these Commandments are not of *human* origin. The tenth Commandment has never been placed on any human statute book! It would be useless to do so, for men could not enforce it. More than any other, perhaps, does *this* Commandment reveal to us *what we are*, the hidden depths of evil within. It is *natural* to *desire* things, even though they belong to others. True; and that only shows the fallen and depraved state of our nature. The last Commandment is especially designed to show men their sinfulness, and their need of a Saviour. Believers, too, are exhorted to 'beware of covetousness' (Luke 12:15). There is only one exception, and that is stated in 1 Corinthians 12:31: 'Covet earnestly *the best gifts*'.

May the Holy Spirit of God fasten these Commandments upon the memory of both writer and reader, and may the fear of God make us tremble before them.

CHAPTER 7

The Restoration of David

His Conviction

An interval of some months elapsed between what is recorded in 2 Samuel 11 and that which is found at the beginning of chapter 12. During this interval David was free to enjoy to the full that which he had acquired through his wrongdoing. The one obstacle which lay in the way of the free indulgence of his passion was removed; Bathsheba was now his. Apparently, the king, in his palace, was secure and immune. So far there had been no intervention of God in judgment, and throughout those months David had remained impenitent for the fearful crimes he had committed. Alas, how dull the conscience of a saint may become. But if David was pleased with the consummation of his vile plans, there was one who was displeased. The eyes of God had marked his evil conduct, and the Divine righteousness would not pass it by. 'These things hast thou done, and I kept silence', yet he adds, 'but I will reprove thee, and set them in order before thine eyes' (Psalm 50:21).

God may suffer his people to indulge the lusts of the flesh and fall into grievous sin, but he will not allow them to remain content and happy in such a case: rather are they made to prove that 'the way of transgressors is hard'. In the 20th chapter of Job, the Holy Spirit has painted a graphic picture of the wretchedness experienced by the evil-doer. 'Though wickedness be sweet in his mouth, though he hide it under his tongue;

though he spare it, and forsake it not, but keep it still within
his mouth; yet his meat in his bowels is turned, *it is the gall
of asps within him*. He hath swallowed down riches, and he
shall vomit them up again: God shall cast them out of his belly.
He shall suck the poison of asps: the viper's tongue shall slay
him... It shall go ill with him that is left of his tabernacle. The
heavens shall reveal his iniquity' (vv 12-16, 26, 27). Notably
is this the case with backsliders, for God will not be mocked
with impugnity.

The coarse pleasures of sin cannot long content a child of
God. It has been truly said that 'Nobody buys a little passing
pleasure in evil at so dear a rate, or keeps it so short a time, as
a good man.' The conscience of the righteous soon reasserts
itself, and makes its disconcerting voice heard. He may yet be
far from true repentance, but he will soon experience keen
remorse. Months may pass before he again enjoys communion with God, but self-disgust will quickly fill his soul. The
saint has to pay a fearfully high price for enjoying 'the
pleasures of sin for a season'. Stolen waters may be sweet for
a moment, but how quickly his 'mouth is filled with gravel'
(Proverbs 20:17). Soon will the guilty one have to cry out, 'he
hath made my chain heavy... he hath made me desolate: he
hath filled me with bitterness... thou hast removed my soul far
off from peace' (Lamentations 3:7, 11, 15, 17).

Though the inspired historian has not described the
wretchedness of David's soul following his murder of Uriah,
yet we may obtain a clear view of the same from the Psalms
penned by him after his conviction and deep contrition. Those
Psalms tell of a sullen closing of his mouth: 'when I kept
silence' (32:3). Though his heart must frequently have smit-
ten him, yet he would not speak to God about his sin; and there

was nothing else he could speak of. They tell of the inward perturbation and tumult that filled him: 'my bones waxed old through *my roaring* all the day long' (32:3): groans of remorse were wrung from his yet unbroken heart. 'For day and night thy hand was heavy upon me' (v 4) - a sense of the Divine holiness and power oppressed him, though it did not melt him.

Even a palace can afford no relief unto one who is filled with bitter remorse. A king may command his subjects, but he cannot quieten the voice of outraged conscience. No matter whether the sun of the morning was shining or the shades of even were falling, there was no escape for David. 'Day and night' God's heavy hand weighed him down: 'my moisture is turned into the drought of summer', he declared (v 4) - it was as though some heated iron was scorching him: all the dew and freshness of his life was dried up. Most probably he suffered acutely in both body and soul.

Thus he dragged through a weary year - ashamed of his guilty dalliance, wretched in his self-accusation, afraid of God, and skulking in the recesses of his palace from the sight of the people.

David learned, what we all learn (and the holier a man is, the more speedily and sharply the lesson follows on the heels of his sin), that every transgression is a blunder, that we never get the satisfaction which we expect from any sin, or if we do, we get something with it which spoils it all. A nauseous drug is added to the exciting, intoxicating drink which temptation offers, and though its flavour is at first disguised by the pleasanter taste of sin, its bitterness is persistent though slow, and clings to the palate long after that has faded away utterly (Alexander Maclaren).

With equal clearness does this appear in the 51st Psalm. 'Restore unto me the joy of thy salvation' (v 12) he cries, for spiritual comforts had entirely deserted him. 'O LORD, open thou my lips: and my mouth shall show forth thy praise' (v 15): the dust had settled upon the strings of his harp because the Spirit within was grieved.

How could it be otherwise? So long as David refused to humble himself beneath the mighty hand of God, seeking from him a spirit of true repentance, and freely confessing his great wickedness, there could be no more peace for him, no more happy communion with God, no further growth in grace. O my reader, we would earnestly press upon you the great importance of *keeping short accounts with God*. Let not guilt accumulate upon thy conscience: make it a point *each* night of spreading before him the sins of the day, and seeking to be cleansed therefrom. Any great sin lying long upon the conscience, unrepented of, or not repented of as the matter requires, only furthers our indwelling corruptions: neglect causes the heart to be hardened. 'My wounds stink and are corrupt *because of my foolishness*' (Psalm 38:5): it was his foolish neglect to make a timely application for the cure of the wounds that sin had made, which he there laments.

At the end of 2 Samuel 11 we read, 'But the thing that David had done displeased the LORD', upon which Matthew Henry says, 'One would think it should be followed that the Lord sent enemies to invade him, terrors to take hold on, and the messengers of death to arrest him. No, he sent *a prophet* to him' - 'And the LORD sent Nathan unto David' (12:1). We are here to behold the exceeding riches of Divine grace and mercy: *such* 'riches' that legal and self-righteous hearts have murmured at, as a making light of sin - so incapable is the natural man of discerning spiritual things: they are 'foolishness' unto him. David had wandered far, but he was not lost. 'Though the righteous fall', yet it is written 'he *shall not be* utterly cast down' (Psalm 37:24). O how tenderly God watches over his sheep! How faithfully he goes after and recovers them, when they have strayed! With what amazing goodness does he heal their backslidings and continue to love them freely!

'And the LORD sent Nathan unto David' (12:1). It is to be duly noted that it was not David who sent for the prophet, though never did he more sorely need his counsel than now. No, it was *God* who took the initiative: it is ever thus, for we never seek him, until he seeks us. It was thus with Moses when a fugitive in Midian, with Elijah when fleeing from Jezebel, with Jonah under the juniper tree, with Peter after his denial (1 Corinthians 15:5). O the marvel of it! How it should melt our hearts. 'If we believe not, yet *he* abideth faithful: he cannot deny himself' (2 Timothy 2:13). Though he says, 'I will visit their transgression with the rod, and their iniquity with stripes', it is at once added, 'Nevertheless my lovingkindness will I not utterly take from him, nor suffer my faithfulness to fail' (Psalm 89:32,33). So it was here: David still had an interest in that everlasting covenant 'ordered in all things and sure' (2 Samuel 23:5).

'And the LORD sent Nathan unto David.' Probably about a year had elapsed from what is recorded in the beginning of the preceding chapter, for the adulterous child was already born (12:14). Rightly did Matthew Henry point out, 'Though God may suffer his people to fall into sin, he will not suffer his people to lie still in it'. No, God will exhibit his holiness, his righteousness, and his mercy in connection therewith. His holiness, by displaying his hatred of the same, and by bringing the guilty one to penitently confess it. His righteousness, in the chastening visited upon it; his mercy, in leading the backslider to forsake it, and then bestow his pardon upon him. What a marvellous and blessed exercise of his varied attributes! 'For the iniquity of his covetousness was I wroth, and smote him: I hid me, and was wroth, and he went frowardly in the way of his heart. I have seen his ways, and will *heal him*(!!): I will lead him also and restore comforts unto him' (Isaiah 58:17, 18).

'And the LORD sent Nathan unto David.' The prophet's task was far from being an enviable one: to meet the guilty king alone, face to face. As yet David had evinced no sign of repentance. God had not cast off his erring child, but he would not condone his grievous offences: all must come out into the light. The Divine displeasure must be made evident: the culprit must be charged and rebuked: David must judge himself, and then discover that where sin had abounded grace did much more abound. Wondrous uniting of Divine right- eousness and mercy - made possible by the cross of Christ! The righteousness of God required that David should be faithfully dealt with; the mercy of God moved him to send Nathan for the recovery of his strayed sheep. 'Mercy and truth are *met together*; righteousness and peace have kissed each other' (Psalm 85:10).

Yes, Nathan might well have quailed before the commis- sion which God now gave him. It was no easy matter to have to rebuke his royal master. Varied indeed are the tasks which the Lord assigns his servants. Often are they sent forth with a message which they well know will be most unpalatable to their hearers; and the temptation to tone it down, to take off its sharp edge, if not to substitute another which will be even more acceptable, is both real and strong. Little do the rank and file even of God's people realise what it costs a minister of the gospel to be *faithful* to his calling. If the apostle Paul felt his need of requesting prayer 'that utterance may be given unto me, that I may open my mouth *boldly*' (Ephesians 6:18, 19), how much more do God's servants today need the support of the supplications of their brethren and sisters in Christ! For on every side the cry now is 'speak unto us *smooth* things'!

On a previous occasion God had sent Nathan to David with a message of promise and comfort (7: 4, 5 etc.); now he is ordered to charge the king with his crimes. He did not decline the unwelcome task, but executed it faithfully. Not only was his mission an unenviable one, but it was far from easy. Few things are more difficult and trying to one with a sensitive disposition than to be called upon to reprove an erring brother. In pondering the method here followed by the prophet - his line of approach to David's slumbering conscience - there is valuable instruction for those of us who may be called upon to deal with similar cases. *Wisdom* from on High (we do not say 'tact', the *world's* term, for more often that word is employed to denote the serpentine subtleties of the serpent than the honest dealings of the Holy Spirit) is sorely needed if we are to be a real help to those who have fallen by the wayside - lest we either condone their offences, or make them despair of obtaining pardon.

Nathan did not immediately charge David with his crimes: instead, he approached his conscience indirectly by means of a *parable* - clear intimation that he was out of communion with God, for he never employed *that* method of revelation with those who were walking in fellowship with him. The method employed by the prophet had the great advantage of presenting the facts of the case before David, *without* stirring up his opposition of self-love and kindling resentment against being directly rebuked; yet causing him to pass sentence

against himself without being aware of it - sure proof that
Nathan had been given wisdom from above!

> There scarcely ever was any thing more calculated, on the one hand,
> to awaken emotions of sympathy, and, on the other, those of
> indignation, than the case here supposed; and the several circum-
> stances by which the heart must be interested in the poor man's case,
> and by which the unfeeling oppression of his rich neighbour was
> aggravated (Thomas Scott).

The prophet began, then, by giving an oblique representation of the vileness of David's offence, which was conveyed
in such a way that the king's judgment was *obliged* to assent
to the gross injustice he was guilty of. The excuselessness, the
heartlessness, and the abominable selfishness of his conduct
was depicted, though Uriah's loyal service and the king's
ingratitude and treachery, and the murder of him and his
fellow-soldiers, was not alluded to - is there not a hint here
that, when reproving an erring brother we should *gradually*
lead up to the worst elements in his offence? Yet obvious as
was the allusion in Nathan's parable, David perceived not its
application unto himself - how this shows that when one is out
of touch with God, he is devoid of spiritual discernment: it is
only in God's light that we can see light!

'And David's anger was greatly kindled against the man,
and he said to Nathan, As the LORD liveth, the man that hath
done this thing shall surely die' (v 5). David supposed that a
complaint was being preferred against one of his subjects.
Forgetful of his own crimes, he was fired with indignation at
the supposed offender, and with a solemn oath condemned
him to death. In condemning the rich man, David unwittingly
condemns himself. What a strange thing the heart of a believer

is! What a medley dwells within it! Often filled with righteous
indignation against the sins of others, while blind to its own!
Real need has each of us to solemnly and prayerfully ponder
the questions of Romans 2:21-23. Self-flattery makes us
quick to mark the faults of others, but blind to our own
grievous sins. Just in proportion as a man is in love with his
own sins and resentful of being rebuked, will he be unduly
severe in condemning those of his neighbours.

Having brought David to pronounce sentence upon a
supposed offender for crimes of far less malignity than his
own, the prophet now, with great courage and plainness,
declared, '*Thou* art the man' (v 7), and speaks directly in the
name of God: 'Thus saith the LORD God of Israel'. First, David
is reminded of the signal favours which had been bestowed
upon him (vv 7, 8), among them the 'wives' or women of
Saul's court, from which he might have selected a wife.
Second, God was willing to bestow yet more (v 8): had he
considered anything was lacking, he might have asked for it,
and had it been for his good the Lord had freely granted it -
cf. Psalm 84:11. Third, in view of God's tender mercies,
faithful love and all-sufficient gifts, he is asked 'Wherefore
hast thou *despised* the commandment of the LORD, to do evil
in his sight?' (v 9). Ah, it is contempt of the Divine authority
which is the occasion of all sin - making light of the Law and
its Giver, acting as though its precepts were mere trifles, and
its threats meaningless.

The desired result was now accomplished. 'And David
said unto Nathan, I have sinned against the LORD' (v 13).
Those words were not uttered lightly or mechanically, as the
sequel shows.

His Repentance

The emperor Arcadius and his wife had a very bitter feeling towards Chrysostom, bishop of Constantinople. One day, in a fit of anger, the emperor said to one of his courtiers. 'I would I were avenged of this bishop!' Several then proposed how this should be done. 'Banish him and exile him to the desert,' said one. 'Put him in prison,' said another. 'Confiscate his property,' said a third. 'Let him die,' said a fourth. Another courtier, whose vices Chrysostom had reproved, said maliciously, 'You all make a great mistake. You will never punish him by such proposals. If banished the kingdom, he will feel God as near to him in the desert as here. If you put him in prison and load him with chains, he will still pray for the poor and praise God in the prison. If you confiscate his property, you merely take away his goods from the poor, not from him. If you condemn him to death, you open heaven to him. Prince, do you wish to be revenged on him? Force him to commit sin. I know him: *this man fears nothing in the world but sin.*' O that this were the only remark which our fellows could pass on you and me, fellow-believer (From the *Fellowship* magazine).

We recently came across the above in our reading, and thought it would form a most suitable introduction to this section. What cause have we *to fear* SIN! - that 'abominable thing' which God hates (Jeremiah 44:4), that horrible disease which brought death into the world (Romans 5:12), that fearful thing which nailed to the cross the Lord of glory (1 Peter 2:24), that shameful thing which fouls the believer's garments and so often brings reproach upon the sacred Name which he bears. Yes, good reason has each of us to *fear* sin, and to beg God that it may please him to work in our hearts a greater horror and hatred of it. Is not this one reason why God permits some of the most eminent saints to lapse into outrageous evils, and place such upon record in his Word: that we should be more distrustful of ourselves, realising that *we* are

liable to the same disgracing of our profession: yea, that we
certainly shall fall into such unless upheld by the mighty hand
of God.

As we have seen David sinned, and sinned grievously.
What was yet worse, for a long season he refused to acknowledge unto God his wickedness. A period of months went by
ere he felt the heinousness of his conduct. Ah, my reader, it
is the inevitable tendency of sin to deaden the conscience and
harden the heart. Therein lies its most hideous feature and
fatal aspect. Sin suggests innumerable excuses to its perpetrator and ever prompts to extenuation. It was thus at the
beginning. When brought face to face with their Maker,
neither Adam nor Eve evidenced any contrition; rather did
they seek to vindicate themselves by placing the blame
elsewhere. Thus it was with each of us whilst in a state of
nature. Sin blinds and hardens, and nought but Divine grace
can illumine and soften. Nothing short of the power of the
Almighty can pierce the calloused conscience or break the
sin-petrified heart.

Now God will not suffer any of his people to remain
indefinitely in a state of spiritual insensibility: sooner or later
he brings to light the hidden things of darkness, convicts them
of their offences, causes them to mourn over the same, and
leads them to repentance. God employs a variety of means in
accomplishing this, for in nothing does he act uniformly. He
is limited to no one measure or method, and being sovereign
he acts as seemeth good unto himself. This may be seen by
comparing some of the cases recorded in the Scriptures. It was
a sense of God's awe-inspiring majesty which brought Job to
repent of his self-righteousness and abhor himself (Job 42:1-
6). It was a vision of the Lord's exalted glory which made

Isaiah cry out, 'Woe is me! for I am undone; because I am a man of unclean lips' (Isaiah 6:1-5). A sight of Christ's miraculous power moved Peter to cry, 'Depart from me, for I am a sinful man, O Lord' (Luke 5:8). Those on the day of Pentecost were 'pricked in their heart' (Acts 2:37) by hearing the apostle's sermon.

In the case of David, God employed *a parable* in the mouth of his prophet to produce conviction. Nathan depicted a case where one was so vilely treated that any who heard the account of it must perforce censure him who was guilty of such an outrage. For though it is the very nature of sin to blind its perpetrator, yet it does not take away his sense of right and wrong. Even when a man is insensible to the enormity of his own transgressions, he is still capable of discerning evil in others: yea, in most instances it seems that the one who has a beam in his own eye is readier to perceive the mote in his fellow's. It was according to this principle that Nathan's parable was addressed to David: if the king was slow to confess his own wickedness, he would be quick enough to condemn like evil in another. Accordingly the case was spread before him.

In the parable (2 Samuel 12:1-4), an appeal is made to both David's affections and his conscience. The position of Uriah and his wife is touchingly portrayed under the figure of a poor man with his 'one little ewe lamb', which was dear to him and 'lay in his bosom'. The one who wronged him is represented as a rich man with 'exceeding many flocks and herd' which greatly heightened his guilt in seizing and slaying the one lone lamb of his neighbour. The occasion of the offence, the temptation to commit it, is stated as 'there came *a traveller* unto the rich man': it was to minister unto *him* that the rich man seized upon the poor man's lamb. That 'traveller' which came to him pictures the restless flesh, the active lusts, the wandering thoughts, the roving eyes of David in connection with Bathsheba. Ah, my reader, it is at *this* point we most need to be upon our guard. 'Casting down imaginations, and every high thing that exalteth itself against the knowledge of God, and bringing into captivity every thought to the obedience of Christ' (2 Corinthians 10:5).

'Keep thy heart with all diligence, for out of it are the issues of life' (Proverbs 4:23). Part of that task lies in regulating our thoughts and repelling unlawful imaginations. True it is that we cannot prevent wandering thoughts from entering our minds nor evil imaginations from surging up within us, but we *are* responsible to resist and reject them. But this is what David failed to do: he *welcomed* this 'traveller', he *entertained* him, he *feasted* him, and feasted him upon that which was *not lawful* - with that which belonged to another: pictured in the parable by the lamb belonging to his neighbour. And, my reader, it is when we give place to our sinful lusts, indulge our evil imaginations, feed our wandering thoughts upon that which is unlawful, that we pave the way for a sad fall. 'Travellers' *will* come to us - the mind will be active - and our responsibility is to see that they are fed with that which is lawful: ponder Philippians 4:8 in this connection.

Nathan, then, traced the trouble back to its source, and showed what it was which occasioned and led up to David's fearful fall. The details of the parable emphasised the excuselessness, the injustice, the lawlessness, the wickedness of his crime. He already had wives of his own, why, then, must he rob poor Uriah of his! The case was so clearly put, the guilt of the offender so evidently established, the king at once

condemned the offender, and said, 'The man that hath done
this thing shall surely die' (12:5). Then it was that the prophet
turned and said to him, '*Thou* art the man'. David did not
flame forth in hot resentment and anger against the prophet's
accusation: he made no attempt to deny his grievous transgression or proffer any excuses for it. Instead, he frankly
owned, 'I have sinned against the LORD' (v 13). Nor were
those words uttered mechanically or lightly as the sequel so
clearly shows, and as we shall now see.

David's slumbering conscience was now awakened, and
he was made to realise the greatness of his guilt. The piercing
arrow from God's quiver, which Nathan had driven into his
diseased heart, opened to David's view the awfulness of his
present case. Then it was that he gave evidence that, though
woeful had been his conduct, nevertheless, he was not a
reprobate soul, totally abandoned by God.

> The dormant spark of Divine grace in David's heart now began to
> rekindle, and before this plain and faithful statement of facts, in the
> name of God, his evasions vanished, and his guilt appeared in all its
> magnitude. He therefore was far from resenting the pointed rebuke
> of the prophet, or attempting any palliation of his conduct: but, in
> deep humiliation of heart, he confessed, 'I have sinned against the
> Lord'. The words are few: but the event proved them to have been
> the language of genuine repentance, which regards sin as committed
> against the authority and glory of the Lord, whether or not it has
> occasioned evil to any fellow-creature (Thomas Scott).

In order to fully obtain the mind of God on any subject
treated of in his Word, Scripture has to be diligently searched
and one passage carefully compared with another - failure to
observe this principle ever results in an inadequate or one-
sided view. It is so here. Nothing is recorded in the historical

account in 2 Samuel about the deep exercises of heart through which David now passed; nothing is said to indicate the reality and depth of his repentance. For *that* we must turn elsewhere, notably to the penitential Psalms. There the Holy Spirit has graciously given us a record of what David was inspired to write thereon, for it is in the Psalms we find most fully delineated the varied experiences of soul through which the believer passes. There we may find an unerring description of every exercise of heart experienced by the saint in his journey through this wilderness scene; which explains why *this* book of Scripture has ever been a great favourite with God's people; therein they find *their own* inward history accurately described.

The two principal Psalms which give us a view of the heart exercises through which David now passed are the 51st and the 32nd. The 51st is evidently the earlier one. In it we see the fallen saint struggling up out of 'the horrible pit and miry clay'. In the latter we behold him standing again on firm ground with a new song in his mouth, even the blessedness of him 'whose sin is covered'. But both of them are evidently to be dated from the time when the sharp thrust of God's lancet in the hand of Nathan pierced David's conscience, and when the healing balsam of God's assurance of forgiveness was laid by the prophet upon his heart. The passionate cries of the sorely-stricken soul (Psalm 51) are really the echo of the Divine promise - the efforts of David's faith to grasp and appropriate the merciful gift of pardon. It was the Divine promise *of* forgiveness which was the basis and encouragement of the prayer *for* forgiveness.

It is to be noted that the title affixed to the 51st Psalm is 'A Psalm of David, when Nathan the prophet came unto him, after he had gone in to Bathsheba.' Beautifully did Spurgeon point out in his introductory remarks, 'When the Divine message had aroused his dormant conscience and made him see the greatness of his guilt, he wrote this Psalm. He had forgotten his psalmody while he was indulging his flesh, but he returned to his harp when his spiritual nature was awakened, and he poured out his song to the accompaniment of sighs and tears.' Great as was David's sin, yet he repented, and was restored. The depths of his anguish and the reality of his repentance are evident in every verse. In it we may behold the grief and the desires of a contrite soul pouring out his heart before God, humbly and earnestly suing for his mercy. Only the Day to come will reveal how many sin-tormented souls have from this Psalm - 'all blotted with the tears in which David sobbed out his repentance' - found a path for backsliders in a great and howling desert.

Although the psalm is one long cry for pardon and restoration, one can discern an order and progress in its petitions - the order, not of an artificial reproduction of a past mood of mind, but the instinctive order in which the emotion of contrite desire will ever pour itself forth. In the psalm all begins (v 1), as all begins in fact, with the grounding of the cry for favour on 'thy loving-kindness', the multitude of thy tender mercies'; the one plea that avails with God, whose love is its own motive and its own measure, whose past acts are the standard for all his future, whose own compassions, in their innumerable numbers, are more than the sum of our transgressions, though these be 'more than the hairs of our head'. Beginning with God's mercy, the penitent soul can learn to look next upon its own sin in all its aspects of evil (Alexander Maclaren).

The depth and intensity of the Psalmist's loathing of self is clearly revealed by the various terms he uses to designate his crime. He speaks of his 'transgressions' (vv 1, 3), and of

his 'iniquity' and 'sin' (vv 2, 3). As another has forcibly
pointed out, 'Looked at in one way, he sees the separate acts
of which he had been guilty - his lust, fraud, treachery,
murder; looked at in another, he seems them all knotted
together in one inextricable tangle of forked, hissing tongues,
like the serpent-locks that coil and twist round a Gorgon head.
No sin dwells alone; the separate acts have a common root,
and the whole is matted together like the green growth on a
stagnant pond, so that, by whatever filament it is grasped the
whole mass is drawn toward you.'

A profound insight into the essence and character of sin is
here exhibited by the accumulated synonyms. It is *transgression*, or as the Hebrew word might be rendered 'rebellion' -
not merely the breach of an impersonal law, but the revolt of
a subject's will against its true King; disobedience to God, as
well as contravention of a standard. It is *iniquity* - perversion
or distortion - acting unjustly or dealing crookedly. It is *sin* or
'missing the mark', for all sin is a blunder, shooting wide of
the true goal, whether regard be had for God's glory or our
own wellbeing and happiness. It is pollution and filth, from
which nothing but atoning blood can cleanse. It is *evil* (v 4),
a vile thing which deserves only unsparing condemnation. It
is a fretting leprosy, causing him to cry, 'Purge me with
hyssop, and I shall be clean; wash me, and I shall be whiter
than snow' (v 7).

'Against thee, thee only, have I sinned, and done this evil
in thy sight' (v 4). In these words David gives evidence of the
sincerity of his contrition and proof that he was a regenerate
man. It is only those possessing a spiritual nature that will
view sin in the presence of God. The evil of all sin lies in its
opposition to God, and a contrite heart is filled with a sense

of the wrong done unto him. Evangelical repentance mourns
for sin because it has displeased a gracious God and dishonoured a loving Father. David, then, was not content with
looking upon his evil in itself, or in relation only to the people
who had suffered by it. He had been guilty of crimes against
Bathsheba and Uriah, and even Joab whom he made his tool,
as well as against all his subjects; but dark as these crimes
were, they assumed their true character only when seen as
committed *against God*.

'Behold, I was shapen in iniquity, and in sin did my mother
conceive me' (v 5). Many have been puzzled by this verse in
the light of its setting, yet it should occasion no difficulty.
Certainly it was not said by David in self-extenuation; rather was
it to emphasise his own excuseless guilt. From the second half
of verse 4 it is plain that he was vindicating God: *thou* hadst
nothing to do with my sin: it was all *mine* own - out of the
proneness unto evil of my depraved nature. It was not thou, but
my own evil lusts, which tempted me. David was engaged in
making *full* confession, and therefore did he acknowledge the
defilement of his very nature. It was to humble himself, clear
God, and magnify the Divine grace, that David said verse 5.

In the clear light of Psalm 51 we cannot doubt the reality,
the sincerity, nor the depth of David's repentance and broken-
hearted contrition. We close this section with a brief quotation
from Thomas Scott:

> Let not any vile hypocrite, who resembles David in nothing but
> his transgressions, and who adds the habit of allowed sin to all
> other aggravations, buoy up his confidence with *his* example: let
> him first imitate David's humiliation, repentance, and other
> eminent graces, before he thinks himself, or requires others to
> consider him as a backslider.

His Forgiveness

The inward experience of a believer consists very largely of growing discoveries of his own vileness and of God's goodness, of his own excuseless failures and of God's infinite forbearance, with a frequent alternation between gloom and joy, confession and thanksgiving. Consequently, the more he reads and meditates upon the Word, the more he sees how exactly suited it is to his case, and how accurately his own checkered history is described therein. The two leading themes of Scriptures are *sin and grace*: throughout the Sacred Volume each of these is traced to its original source, each is delineated in its true character, each is followed out in its consequences and ends, each is illustrated and exemplified by numerous personal examples. Strange as it first sounds, yet it is true that, upon these two, *sin and grace*, do turn all the transactions between God and the souls of men.

The force of what has just been said receives clear and striking demonstration in the case of David. Sin in all its hideousness is seen at work within him, plunging him into the mire; but grace is also discovered in all its loveliness, delivering and cleansing him. The one serves as a dark background from which the other may shine forth the more gloriously. Nowhere do we behold so unmistakably the fearful nature and horrible works of sin than in the man after God's own heart, so signally favoured and so highly honoured, yet failing so ignominiously and sinking so low. Yet nowhere do we behold so vividly the amazing grace of God as in working true repentance in this notorious transgressor, pardoning his iniquity, and restoring him to communion. King Saul was rejected for a far milder offence: ah, *he* was not in the covenant! O the awe-inspiring sovereignty of Divine grace.

Not only has the Holy Spirit faithfully recorded the awful details of David's sin. He has also fully described the heart-affecting repentance of the contrite king. In addition thereto, he has shown us how David sought and obtained the Divine forgiveness. Each of these is recorded for our learning, and, we may add, for our comfort. The first shows us the fearful tendency of the flesh which still indwells the believer, with its proneness to produce the vilest fruit. The second makes known to us the lamentable work which we make for ourselves when we indulge our lusts, and the bitter cup we shall then be obliged to drink. The third informs us that grievous though our case be, yet it is not hopeless, and reveals the course which God requires us to follow. Having already considered the first two at some length, we will now turn to the third.

As it is in the Psalms that the Spirt has recorded the exercises of David's broken heart, so it is therein we learn of how he obtained the Divine pardon for his aggravated offences. We will begin by turning to one of the last of the 'penitential' Psalms, which we believe was probably penned by David himself. 'Out of the depths have I cried unto thee, O LORD' (130:1). There are various 'depths' into which God suffers his people, at times, to fall: 'depths' of trial and trouble over financial losses, family bereavements, personal illness. There are also 'depths' of sin and guilt, into which they may plunge themselves, with the consequent 'depths' of conviction and anguish, of darkness and despair - through the hidings of God's face, and of Satanic opposition and despondency. It is these which are here more particularly in view.

The design of the Holy Spirit in this 130th Psalm was to express and represent in the person and conduct of the psalmist the case of a soul entangled in the meshes of Satan, overwhelmed by the conscious guilt of sin, but relieved by a discovery of the grace of God, with its deportment upon and participation of that grace. We quote the helpful paraphrase of John Owen in its opening verses:

O Lord, through my manifold sins and provocation I have brought myself into great distresses. Mine iniquities are always before me, and I am ready to be overwhelmed with them, as with a flood of waters; for they have brought me into depths, wherein I am ready to be swallowed up. But yet, although my distress be great and perplexing, I do not, I dare not, utterly despond and cast away all hopes of relief or recovery. Nor do I seek unto any other remedy, way, or means of relief, but I apply myself to thee, Jehovah, to thee alone. And in this my application unto thee, the greatness and urgency of my troubles makes my soul urgent, earnest, and pressing in my supplication. Whilst I have no rest, I can give thee no rest; oh, therefore, attend and hearken unto the voice of my crying!

When the soul is in such a case - in the 'depths' of distress and despondency - there is no relief for it *but in God*, fully unburdening the heart to him. The soul cannot rest in such a state, and no deliverance is to be obtained from any creature helps. 'Asshur shall not save us; we will not ride upon horses: neither will we say any more to the work of our hands, Ye are our gods: for *in thee* the fatherless (the grief-stricken and helpless) findeth mercy' (Hosea 14:3). In God alone is help to be found. The vain things which deluded Romanists have invented - prayers 'to the Virgin', penances, confession to 'priests', fastings, masses, pilgrimages, works of compensation - are all 'cisterns which hold no water'. Equally useless are the counsels of the world to sin-distressed souls - to try a change of scenery, diversion from work, music, cheerful

society, pleasure, etc. There is no peace but in the God of
peace.

Now in his very lowest state the Psalmist *sought help* from
the Lord, nor was his appeal in vain. And this is what *we* need
to lay hold of when in similar circumstances: it is recorded to
this very end. Dear Christian reader, however deplorable may
be your condition, however dire your need, however desper-
ate your situation, however intolerable the load on your
conscience, your case *is not hopeless*. David cried, and was
heard; he sought mercy, and obtained it; and the Divine
promise to you and me is, 'Let us therefore come boldly unto
the Throne of Grace, that we may *obtain mercy*, and find grace
to help in time of need' (Hebrews 4:16). David was not the
only one who cried unto God out of 'the depths'. Think of the
prophet Jonah: following a course of self-will, deliberately
fleeing from God's commandment, then cast into the sea and
swallowed by the whale: yet of him too we read, 'I cried by
reason of mine affliction unto the Lord, and he heard me; out
of the belly of hell cried I, and thou *heardest* my voice' (2:2).

It was his hope in the plenitude of Divine grace that moved
David to seek unto the Lord. 'If thou, Lord, shouldest mark
iniquities, O Lord, who shall stand? But there is forgiveness
with thee, that thou mayest be feared. I wait for the Lord, my
soul doth *wait*, and in his word do I *hope*' (Psalm 130:3-5). In
the third verse he owns that he could not stand before the thrice
Holy One on the ground of his own righteousness, and that if
God were to 'mark iniquities', that is, impute them unto
condemnation, then his case was indeed hopeless. In the
fourth verse he humbly reminds God that there *was* forgiveness with him, that he might be revered and adored - not trifled
with and mocked, for Divine pardon is not a licence for future

self-indulgence. In the fifth verse he hopefully waits for some 'token for good' (Psalm 86:17), some 'answer of peace' (Genesis 41:16) from the Lord.

But it is in the 51st Psalm that we find David most definitely and most earnestly suing for God's pardon. The same intensity of feeling expressed in the use of so many words for sin, is revealed also in his reiterated synonyms for pardon. This petition comes from his lips again and again, not because he thought to be heard for his much speaking, but because of the earnestness of his longing. *Such* repetitions are signs of the persistence of faith, while those which last, like the prayers of Baal's priests 'from morning till the time of evening sacrifice', indicate only the supplicant's doubts. The 'vain repetition' against which the Lord warned, is not a matter of repeating the same form of request, but of mechanically multiplying the same - like the Romanist with his 'pater nosters' - and supposing there is virtue and merit in so doing.

David prayed that his sins might be *blotted out* (v 1), which petition conceives of them as being recorded against him. He prayed that he might be *washed* (v 2) from them, in which they are felt to be foul stains, which require for their removal hard scrubbing and beating - for such is, according to some of the commentators, the force of the Hebrew verb. He prayed that he might be *cleansed* (v 7) which was the technical word for the priestly cleansing of the leper, declaring him clear of the taint. There is a touching appropriateness in this last reference, for not only lepers, but those who had become defiled by contact with a dead body, were thus purified (Numbers 19); and on whom did the taint of this corruption cleave as on the murderer of Uriah? The prayer in the original is even more remarkable, for the verb is formed from the word for 'sin', and if our language permitted it, would be rendered, 'thou shalt *un-sin* me.'

'Create in me a clean heart, O God, and renew a right spirit within me' (Psalm 51:10). His sin had made manifest his weakness and sensuality, but his remorse and anguish evidenced that above and beyond all other desires was his abiding longing after God. The petitions of this Psalm clearly demonstrate that, despite his weakness and Satan's victory over him, yet the root of the Divine matter was in David. In asking God to *create* in him a clean heart, David was humbly placing himself on a level with the unregenerate: he realised too his own utter inability to quicken or renew himself - God alone can create either a new heart or a new earth. In asking for a right spirit, he was owning that God takes account of the state of our souls as well as the quality of our actions: a '*right* spirit' is a loving, trustful, obedient, steadfast one, that none but God can either impart or maintain.

In the midst of his abased confessions and earnest cries for pardon, there comes with wondrous force and beauty the bold request for restoration to full communion: 'Restore unto me the joy of thy salvation' (v 12). How that request evidenced a more than ordinary confidence in the rich mercy of God, which would efface all the consequences of his sin! But note well *the position* occupied by this petition: it *followed* his request for pardon and purity - apart from *these*, 'joy' would be nought but vain presumption or insane enthusiasm. 'And uphold me by thy free Spirit' (v 12). First, he had prayed, 'Take not thy Holy Spirit from me' (v 11) - an obvious reference to the awful judgment which fell upon his predecessor, Saul; here, assured that the previous petition is granted, and conscious of his own weakness and inability to stand, he asks to be supported by that One who alone can impart and maintain holiness.

Ere passing on to consider the gracious answer which David received, perhaps this is the best place to consider the question, Was he justified in asking God *for* forgiveness? Or to put it in a form which may better satisfy the critical, Are we warranted in supplicating God for the pardon of our sins? For there are those today who insist that we occupy a different and superior relation to God than David did. It will no doubt surprise some of our readers that we raise such a question. One would naturally think it was so evident that we *ought* to pray for forgiveness that none would question it; that such a prayer is so well founded upon Scripture itself, is so agreeable to our condition as erring believers, and is so honouring to God that we *should* take the place of penitent suppliants, acknowledging our offences and seeking his pardoning mercy, that no further proof is required. But alas, so great is the confusion in Christendom today, and so much error abounds, that we feel obliged to devote one or two paragraphs unto the elucidation of this point.

There is a group, more or less influential, who argue that it is dishonouring to the blood of Christ for any Christian to ask God to pardon his sins, quoting 'having forgiven you *all* trespasses' (Colossians 2:13). These people confuse the impetration of the Atonement with its application, or in less technical terms, what Christ purchased for his people with the Holy Spirit's making good the same to them in the court of their conscience. Let it be clearly pointed out that, in asking God for forgiveness, we do *not* pray as though the blood of Christ had never been shed, or as though *our* tears and prayers could make any compensation to Divine justice. Nevertheless, renewed sins call for renewed repentance: true, we do not then need another Redeemer, but we *do* need a fresh exercise of Divine mercy toward us (Hebrews 4:16), and a fresh application to our conscience of the cleansing blood (1 John 1:7, 9).

The saints of old prayed for pardon: 'For thy name's sake, O LORD, pardon mine iniquity: for it is great' (Psalm 25:11). The Lord Jesus taught his disciples *to pray* 'Forgive us our debts' (Matthew 6:12), and that prayer is assuredly for Christians today, for it is addressed to '*our Father*'! In praying for forgiveness we ask God to be gracious to us for *Christ*'s sake; we ask him *not* to lay such sins to our charge - 'And enter not into judgment with thy servant' (Psalm 143:2); we ask him for a gracious *manifestation* to us of his mercy to our conscience - 'Make me *to hear* joy and gladness; that the bones which thou hast broken may rejoice' (Psalm 51:8); we ask him for the comforting proofs of his forgiveness, that we may again have 'the joy of his salvation'.

Now it is in the 32nd Psalm that we learn of the answer which 'the God of all grace' (1 Peter 5:10) granted unto his erring but penitent child. In his introductory remarks thereon Spurgeon said, 'Probably his deep repentance over his great sin was followed by such blissful peace that he was led to pour out his spirit in the soft music of this choice song.' The word 'Maschil' at its head signifies 'Teaching'. 'The experience of one believer affords rich instruction to others, it reveals the footsteps of the flock, and so comforts and directs the weak.' At the close of the 51st Psalm David had prayed, 'O LORD, open thou my lips, and my mouth shall show forth thy praise' (v 15): here the prayer has been heard, and this is the beginning of the fulfilment of his vow.

'*Blessed* is he whose transgression is forgiven, whose sin is covered. Blessed is the man unto whom the LORD imputeth not iniquity, and in whose spirit there is no guile' (Psalm 32:1, 2). In the former Psalm David had begun with the plaintive cry for mercy; here he opens with a burst of praise, celebrating the happiness of the pardoned penitent. There we heard the sobs of a man in the agonies of contrition and abasement; here we have an account of their blessed issue. There we had the multiplied synonyms for sin and for the forgiveness which was desired; here is the many-sided preciousness of forgiveness *possessed*, which runs over in various yet equivalent phrases. The one is a psalm of wailing; the other, to use its own words, a 'song of deliverance'.

The joy of conscious pardon sounds out in the opening '*Blessed* is the man', and the exuberance of his spirit rings forth in the melodious variations of the one thought of forgiveness in the opening words. How gratefully he draws on the treasures of his recent experience, which he sets forth as the *taking away* of sin - the removal of an intolerable load from his heart; as the *covering* of sin - the hiding of its hideousness from the all-seeing Eye by the blood of Christ; as the *imputing not* of sin - a debt discharged. How blessed the realisation that his own forgiveness would encourage other penitent souls - '*For this* shall every one that is godly pray unto thee' (v 6). Finally, how precious the deep assurance which enables the restored one to say, 'Thou art my hiding place; thou shalt preserve me from trouble; thou shalt compass me about with songs of deliverance' (v 7)!

Here, then, is hope for the greatest backslider, if he will but humble himself before the God of all grace. True sorrow *for* sin is followed by the pardon *of* sin: 'If we confess our sins, he is faithful and just to forgive us our sins, and to cleanse us from all unrighteousness' (1 John 1:9).

Is it possible that such a backslider from God can be recovered, and admitted afterwards to comfortable communion with him? Doubtless it is: 'for with the Lord there is mercy, and with him there is plenteous redemption', and he will never cast out one humble penitent believer, whatever his former crimes have been, nor suffer Satan to pluck any of his sheep out of his hand. Let then those who are fallen return to the Lord without delay, and seek forgiveness through the Redeemer's atoning blood (Thomas Scott).

CHAPTER 8

Elisha's Testings

The peculiar relation which existed between Elijah and Elisha foreshadowed that which pertains to Christ and his servants, and the early experiences through which Elisha passed are those which almost every genuine minister of the gospel is called upon to encounter. All the preliminary details recorded of the prophet before his mission commenced must have their counterpart in the early history of any who are used of God in the work of his kingdom. Those experiences in the case of Elisha began with a definite call from the Lord, and that is still his order of procedure. That call was followed by a series of very real testings, which may well be designated as a preliminary course of discipline. Those testings were many and varied. There were seven in number, which at once indicates the thoroughness and completeness of the ordeals through which Elisha went and by which he was schooled for the future.

(1) The testing of his affections
This occurred at the time he received his call to devote the whole of his time and energies to the service of God and his people. A stern test it was. Elisha was not one who had failed in temporal matters and now desired to 'better his position', nor was he deprived of those who cherished him and was therefore anxious to enter a more congenial circle. Far from

it. He was the son of a well-to-do farmer, living with parents to whom he was devotedly attached. Response to Elijah's casting of the prophetic mantle upon him meant not only the giving up of favourable worldly prospects, but the severing of happy home ties. The issue was plainly drawn: which should dominate - zeal for Jehovah or love for his parents? That Elisha was very far from being one of a cold and unfeeling disposition is clear from a number of things. When Elijah bade him remain at Bethel, he replied, 'I will not leave thee' (2 Kings 2:2); and when his master was caught away from him, he evidenced his deep grief by crying out, 'My father! My father!' and by rending his garments asunder (v 12).

No, Elisha was no stoic, and it cost him something to break away from his loved ones. But he shrank not from the sacrifice demanded of him. He 'left the oxen' with which he had been ploughing and 'ran after Elijah' asking only, 'Let me, I pray thee, kiss my father and my mother, and I will follow thee' (1 Kings 19:20). When permission was granted, a hasty farewell speech was made and he took his departure; and the sacred narrative contains no mention that he ever returned home even for a brief visit. Dutiful respect, yea, tender regard, was shown for his parents, but he did not prefer them before God. The Lord does not require his servants to callously ignore their filial duty, but he does claim the first place in their hearts. Unless one who is contemplating an entrance into the ministry is definitely prepared to accord him that, he should at once abandon his quest. No man is eligible for the ministry unless he is ready to resolutely subordinate natural ties to spiritual bonds. Blessedly did the spirit prevail over the flesh in Elisha's response to this initial trial.

(2) The testing of his sincerity

This occurred at the outset of the final journey of the two prophets. 'And it came to pass when the LORD would take up Elijah into heaven by a whirlwind that Elijah went with Elisha from Gilgal. And Elijah said unto Elisha, Tarry here I pray thee' (2 Kings 2:1-2). Various reasons have been advanced by commentators as to why the Tishbite should have made such a request. Some think it was because he wished to be alone, that modesty and humility would not suffer that his companion should witness the very great honour which was about to be bestowed upon him. Others suppose it was because he desired to spare Elisha the grief of a final leave-taking. But in view of all that follows, and taking this detail in connection with the whole incident, we believe these words of the prophet bear quite a different interpretation, namely, that Elijah was now making proof of Elisha's determination and attachment to him. At the time of his call Elisha had said, 'I will follow thee', and now he was given the opportunity to go back if he were so disposed.

There was one who accompanied the apostle Paul for a while, but later he had to lament, 'Demas hath forsaken me, having loved this present world, and is departed unto Thessalonica' (2 Timothy 4:10). Many have done likewise. Daunted by the difficulties of the way, discouraged by the unfavourable response to their efforts, their ardour cooled, and they concluded they had mistaken their calling; or, because only small and unattractive fields opened to them, they decided to better themselves by returning to worldly employment. To what numbers do those solemn words of Christ apply: 'No man, having put his hand to the plough, and looking back, is fit for the kingdom of God' (Luke 9:62). Far otherwise was it with Elisha. No fleeting impression had actuated him when he declared to Elijah, 'I will follow thee.' And when he was put to the test as to whether or not he was prepared to follow him to the end of the course, he successfully gave evidence of his unwavering fidelity. 'As the LORD liveth, and as thy soul liveth, I will not leave thee' was his unflinching response. Oh for like stability.

(3) The testing of his will or resolution

From Gilgal, Elijah and his companion had gone on to Bethel, and there he encountered a subtle temptation, one which had prevailed over any whose heart was not thoroughly established. 'And the sons of the prophets that were at Beth-el came forth to Elisha and said unto him, Knowest thou that the LORD will take away thy master from thy head today?' (2 Kings 2:3). Which was as much as saying, Why think of going on any further, what is the use of it, when the Lord is on the point of taking him from you? And mark it well, they who here sought to make him waver from his course were not the agents of Jezebel but those who were on the side of the Lord. Nor was it just one who would deter Elisha, but apparently the whole body of the prophets endeavoured to persuade him that he should relinquish his purpose. It is in this very way God tries the mettle of his servants: to make evident to themselves and others whether they are vacillating or steadfast, whether they are regulated wholly by his call and will or whether their course is directed by the counsels of men.

A holy independence should mark the servant of God. Thus it was with the chief of the apostles: 'I conferred not with flesh and blood' (Galatians 1:16). Had he done so, what trouble would he have made for himself; had he listened to the

varied advice the other apostles would offer, what a state of
confusion his own mind would have been in! If Christ is my
Master, then it is from him, and from him alone, I must take
my orders. Until I am sure of his will I must continue to wait
upon him; once it is clear to me, I must set out on the
performance of it, and nothing must move me to turn aside.
So it was here. Elisha had been Divinely called to follow
Elijah, and he was determined to cleave to him unto the end,
even though it meant going against well-meant advice and
offending the whole of his fellows. 'Hold ye your peace' was
his reply. This was one of the trials which this writer encountered many years ago, when his pastor and Christian friends
urged him to enter a theological seminary, though they knew
that deadly error was taught there. It was not easy to take his
stand against them, but he is deeply thankful he did so.

(4) The testing of his faith

'And Elijah said unto him, Elisha, tarry here, I pray thee; for
the LORD hath sent me to Jericho' (2 Kings 2:4). 'Tarry here.'
They were at Bethel, and this was a place of sacred memories.
It was here that Jacob had spent his first night as he fled from
the wrath of his brother. Here he had been favoured with that
vision of the ladder whose top reached unto heaven and beheld
the angels of God ascending and descending on it. Here it was
Jehovah had revealed himself and given him precious promises. When he awakened, Jacob said, 'Surely the LORD is in
this place... this is none other but the house of God and this is
the gate of heaven' (Genesis 28). Delectable spot was this: the
place of divine communion. Ah, one which is supremely
attractive to those who are spiritually minded, and therefore
one which such are entirely loath to leave. What can be more

desirable than to abide where such privileges and favours are enjoyed! So felt Peter on the holy mount. As he beheld Christ transfigured and Moses and Elijah talking with him, he said, 'Lord, it is good for us to be here: if thou wilt let us make here three tabernacles; one for thee, and one for Moses and one for Elijah.' Let us remain and enjoy such blessing. But that could not be.

God still tests his servants at this very point. They are in some place where the smile of heaven manifestly rests upon their labours. The Lord's presence is real, his secrets are revealed to them, and intimate communion is enjoyed with him. If he followed his own inclinations he would remain there, but he is not free to please himself: he is the servant of another and must do his bidding. Elijah had announced, 'The LORD hath sent me to Jericho' and if Elisha were to 'follow' him to the end then to Jericho he too must go. True, Jericho was far less attractive than Bethel, but the will of God pointed clearly to it. It is not the consideration of his own tastes and comforts which is to actuate the minister of Christ but the performance of duty, no matter where it leads to. The mount of transfiguration made a powerful appeal unto Peter, but at the base thereof there was a demon-possessed youth in dire need of deliverance! (Matthew 17:14-18). Elisha resisted the tempting prospect, saying again, 'I will not leave thee.' Oh, for such fidelity!

(5) The testing of his patience
This was a twofold test. When the two prophets arrived at Jericho, the younger one suffered a repetition of what he had experienced at Bethel. Once again 'the sons of the prophets' from the local school accosted him, saying, 'Knowest thou

--

that the LORD will take away thy master from thy head today?'
Elijah himself they left alone, but his companion was set upon
by them. It is the connection in which this occurs that supplies
the key to its meaning. The whole passage brings before us
Elisha being tested first in one way and at one point and then
at another. That he should meet with a repetition at Jericho of
what he had encountered at Bethel is an intimation that the
servant of God needs to be especially on his guard at this point.
He must not put his trust even in 'princes', temporal or
spiritual, but cease entirely from man, trusting in the Lord and
leaning not on his own understanding. Though it was annoy-
ing to be pestered thus by these men, Elisha made them a
courteous reply, yet one which showed them he was not to be
turned away from his purpose: 'Yea, I know it, hold ye your
peace.'

'And Elijah said unto him, Tarry, I pray thee, here; for the
LORD hath sent me to Jordan.' This he said to prove him, as the
Saviour tested the two disciples on the way to Emmaus, when
he 'made as though he would have gone further' (Luke
24:28). Much ground had been traversed since they had set out
together from Gilgal. Was Elisha growing tired of the journey, or was he prepared to persevere to the end? How many
grow weary of well doing and fail to reap because they faint.
How many fail at this point of testing and drop out when
Providence appears to afford them a favourable opportunity
of so doing. Elisha might have pleaded, 'I may be of some
service here to the young prophets, but of what use can I be
to Elijah at the Jordan?' Philip was being greatly used of God
in Samaria (Acts 8:12) when the angel of the Lord bade him
arise and go south 'unto Gaza, which is desert' (v 26). And he
arose and went, and God honoured his obedience. And Elisha

said to his master, 'I will not leave thee,' no, not at the eleventh hour; and great was his reward.

(6) The testing of his character

'And it came to pass, when they were gone over (the Jordan), that Elijah said unto Elisha, Ask what I shall do for thee, before I be taken away from thee' (2 Kings 2:9). Here is clear proof that Elijah had been making trial of his companion when he had at the different stopping places, bade him 'Tarry here' or remain behind, for certainly he would have extended no such an offer as this had Elisha been disobedient and acting in self-will. Clearly the Tishbite was so well pleased with Elisha's devotion and attendance that he determined to reward him with some parting blessing: 'Ask what I shall do for thee.' If this was not the most searching of all the tests, certainly it was the most revealing. What was his heart really set upon? What did he desire above all else? At first glance it seemed surprising that Elijah should fling open so wide a door and offer to supply anything his successor should ask. But not only had they spent several years together; Elisha's reaction to the other testings convinced him that this faithful soul would ask nothing which was incongruous or which God could not give.

'And Elisha said, I pray thee, let a double portion of thy spirit be upon me.' He rose above all fleshly and worldly desires, all that the natural heart would crave, and asked for that which would be most for the glory of God and the good of his people. Elisha sought neither wealth nor honours, worldly power nor prestige. What he asked for was that he might receive that which marked him out as Elijah's first-born, the heir of his official patrimony (Deuteronomy 21:17).

It was a noble request. The work to which he was called involved heavy responsibilities and the facing of grave dangers, and for the discharge of his duties he needed to be equipped with spiritual power. That is what every servant of God needs above everything else: to be 'endued with power from on high'. The most splendid faculties, the ablest intellect, the richest acquirements, count for nothing unless they be energized by the holy one.

The work of the ministry is such that no man is naturally qualified for it; only God can make any meet for the same. For that endowment the apostles waited upon God for ten days. To obtain it Elisha had to successfully endure the previous testings, pass through Jordan and keep his eye fixed steadily upon his master.

(7) The testing of his endowment

When we ask God for something it is often his way to test our earnestness and importunity by keeping us waiting for it, and then when he grants our request, he puts our fidelity to the proof in the use we make of it.

If it is faith that is bestowed, circumstances arise which are apt to call into exercise all our doubts and fears. If it is wisdom which is given, situations soon confront us where we are sorely tempted to give way to folly. If it is courage which is imparted, then perils will have to be faced which are calculated to make the stoutest quake. When we receive some spiritual gift, God so orders things that opportunity is afforded for the exercise of it.

It was thus with Elisha. A double portion of Elijah's spirit was granted him, and the prophetic mantle of his master fell at his feet. What use would he make of it? Suffice it now to say that he was confronted by the Jordan - he was on the wrong side of it, and no longer was there any Elijah to divide asunder its waters!

We turn now from the testings to which Elisha was subjected unto the course which he had to take. The spiritual significance of his journey has also to receive its counterpart in the experiences of the servant of Christ.

That journey began at Gilgal (2 Kings 2:1), and none can work acceptably in the kingdom of God until his soul is acquainted with what that place stands for. It was the first stopping-place of Israel after they entered Canaan, and where they were required to tarry before they set out on the conquest of their inheritance (Joshua 5:9). It was there that all the males who had been born in the wilderness were circumcised.

Now 'circumcision' speaks of separation from the world, consecration to God, and the knife's application to the flesh. Figuratively it stood for the cutting off of the old life, the rolling away of 'the reproach of Egypt'. There is a circumcision 'of the heart' (Romans 2:29), and it is that which is the distinguishing mark of God's spiritual children, as circumcision of the flesh had identified his earthly people.

Gilgal, then, is where the path of God's servant must necessarily begin. Not until he unsparingly mortifies the flesh, separates from the world, and consecrates himself unreservedly to God is he prepared to journey further.

From Gilgal Elisha passed on to 'Bethel', which means 'the house of God'. As we have seen, it was originally the place of hallowed memories, but in the course of time it had been grievously defiled. Bethel had been horribly polluted; for it was there that Jeroboam set up one of his golden calves, appointed an idolatrous priesthood, and led the people into terrible sin (1 Kings 12:28, 33). Elisha must visit this place so that he might be suitably affected with the dishonour done unto the Lord.

History has repeated itself. The house of God, the professing church, is defiled, and the servant of Christ must take to heart the apostate condition of Christendom today if his ministry is to be effective. From Bethel they proceeded to Jericho, a place that was under God's curse (Joshua 6:26). The servant of God needs to enter deeply into the solemn fact that this world is under the curse of a holy God. And what is that 'curse'? Death (Romans 6:23), and it is of that the Jordan (the final stopping-place) speaks. That too must be passed through in the experience of his soul if the minister is to be effective.

CHAPTER 9

Christian Submission

Submitting yourselves one to another, in the fear of God
(Ephesians 5:21).

This is a general exhortation which sums up much of what has
been set forth in the fourth and fifth chapters of this epistle.
It is founded upon the grand truth of the unity of the mystical
Body of Christ, being addressed to the saints in whom, as
living members of that Body, in the building up of which they
are both individually interested and personally responsible,
according to the measure of grace bestowed upon each (4:1-
7, 16). When bidding them 'speak every man truth with his
neighbour', it was at once added '*for* we are members one of
another' (4:25). Holding firmly to the head by faith, they were
to walk in the power of that Spirit who secured them in Christ
for salvation and joined them to each other in his love (5:18-
20). Above all, it was to be kept in their remembrance that
corporately they were God's 'temple' (2:19-21) and individually his 'children' (5:1), and so were exhorted to 'walk in love'
(5:2) and 'in the fear of God'. Therefore they should submit
themselves not only to God in their individual relation to him,
but also to one another.

Ephesians 5:21 is also to be regarded as standing at the head
of that section of the epistle which runs on to the end of 6:9,
enunciating the general principle which is illustrated by the

details of the verses that follow. 'Submitting yourselves one to another' certainly does not signify that true Christianity is a species of spiritual communism, which reduces all to one common level. So far from breaking up the ordinary relations of life and producing disorder, lawlessness and insubordination, it confirms every legitimate authority and makes each just yoke lighter.

> Let every soul be subject unto the higher powers. For there is no power but of God: the powers that be are ordained of God... Render therefore to all their dues: tribute to whom tribute, custom to whom custom, fear to whom fear, honour to whom honour (Romans 13:1, 7).

> Obey them that have the rule over you, and submit yourselves, for they watch for your souls, that they may give account, that they may do it with joy and not with grief (Hebrews 13:17).

> Fear God, honour the king (1 Peter 2:17).

'Submitting yourselves one to another': according to your different situations and relations in the church and in the community, and that subjection which is established by God's Word and ordered by his providence.

This call to mutual subjection then, not only crowns the series of precepts going before, but is also made the foundation of an exposition of Christian deportment in those natural and social relations to which special obligations belong, and in which Christians are likely to find themselves placed. The gospel does not abolish civil distinctions, but binds the believer unto a keeping of the order set up by God.

In the light of what immediately follows, where wives are enjoined to be in subjection to their husbands, children to their parents, and servants to their masters, some have concluded

that 'submitting yourselves one to another' signifies nothing
more than 'render obedience unto whom it is due'. But it is an
unwarrantable narrowing of its scope to restrict it unto the
duty of inferiors to superiors, for the terms of this injunction
are not qualified. Nor does such a limitation accord so well
with other Scriptures. But more: such an interpretation is not
in keeping with what follows, for husbands, parents, masters,
are also addressed and *their duties* pressed upon them.

While the duty of the wife's subjection to her husband is
insisted upon, yet the obligations of the husband to his wife
are also enforced. If children be there required to render
obedience to their parents, the responsibility of fathers is also
stated. While servants are instructed how to conduct themselves unto their masters, the latter are taught to treat their
employees with due consideration and kindness. There too the
balance is blessedly preserved. Power is not to be abused.
Authority must not degenerate into tyranny. Law is to be
administered mercifully. Rule is to be regulated by love.
Government and discipline must be maintained in the state,
the church, and the home; yet governors are to act in the fear
of God, and instead of domineering over their subjects, seek
their good and serve their interests.

Christians are not to aspire after dominance but usefulness.
Self-denial rather than self-assertiveness is the badge of
Christian discipleship. Saints are likened unto sheep and not
goats or wolves. Submitting yourselves one to another means
mutually serving one another, seeking each other's wellbeing
and advantage in all things.

'Sin is the transgression of the law' (1 John 3:24): that is
to say, sin is a revolt against God's authority, a defying of him,
a species of self-will. Sin chafes at any restraints, determined

to have its own way. Sin is self-centred, imperious, indifferent
to the welfare of others. Yokes and restrictions are intolerable
unto sin, and every attempt to enforce them meets with
opposition. That resistance is evinced from earliest infancy,
for a thwarted babe will cry and kick because not suffered to
have its own way. Because all are born in sin the world is filled
with strife and contention, crime and war. But at regeneration
a principle of grace is communicated, and though sin be not
annihilated, its dominion is broken. The love of God is shed
abroad in the renewed heart to counteract its native selfishness. The yoke of Christ is voluntarily assumed by the
believer and his example becomes the rule of his daily walk.
Made a member of Christ's body, he is henceforth to lay
himself out in promoting the interests of his brethren and
sisters. He is under bonds to do good unto all men, especially
to those who belong to the Household of Faith.

It is because sin indwells the Christian, he needs to have
this injunction 'submitting yourselves one to another' frequently pressed upon him. Such is poor human nature that
when a man is elevated to a position of honour, even though
it be a regenerate man who is called to serve as a deacon, he
is prone to lord it over his brethren. A most solemn warning
against this horrible proclivity is found in Luke 22:24. 'And
there was also a strife among them, which of them should be
accounted the greatest.' That strife was among the twelve
apostles, while they sat in the Saviour's presence, after the
Supper! Alas, how little has that warning been heeded! How
many since then have aspired for the precedency. How often
a spirit of envy and strife has been engendered by those who
strove for superiority in the churches. How few realise that
doing good is better than being great, or rather, that the only

true and noble greatness consists in being good and doing
good - to spend and be spent in the service of others. Greatness
is not being toadied unto, but ministering to those less
favoured.

Nevertheless, there *is* a subordination and condescension
appointed by God which we are required to observe. This is
true of *ecclesiastical power*. God has ordained that there shall
be teachers and taught, governors and governed. He raises up
those who are to have the supervision of others, and they are
required to subordinate themselves to their authority (Hebrews 13:17). But their rule is administrative and not legislative,
directive more than authoritative, and 'managed by a council
rather than a court' as Manton expresses it.

Here too there must be *mutual* submission, for in both
governors and governed there is mutual service. The governors themselves are but 'ministers' (1 Corinthians 4:1): they
have indeed an honourable office, yet they are only *servants*
(2 Corinthians 4:5), whose work is to feed the flock, to act as
directors or guides by word and example (1 Timothy 4:12).
Though they 'are over you in the Lord' (1 Thessalonians
5:12), yet not 'as being lords over God's heritage' (1 Peter
5:5) but as motivated by love for souls, seeking their edifica-
tion, gently endeavouring to persuade rather than compelling
and tyrannizing.

There is also a *political power*, or governmental authority,
in the civil state, which is God's ordinance and unto which his
people must yield for his sake. 'Submit yourselves to every
ordinance of man for the Lord's sake: whether it be to the king
as supreme; or unto governors, as unto them that are sent by
him for the punishment of evildoers, and for the praise of them
that do well' (1 Peter 2:12, 13). Thus there is an obligation of

conscience to submit unto our civil governors, both unto the supreme and the subordinate magistrate, the only exception being when they require something from me which clashes with God's Rule, for to act contrary to *that* would be defiance of Divine authority, and therefore would be for the Devil's sake rather than the Lord's. Honour, subordination, obedience is due unto the ministers of state, nevertheless they in turn are under the Divine dominion, 'for he is the *minister* of God to thee for good' (Romans 13:4). The magistrate, the member of the cabinet (or senate), the king himself, is but the servant of God, to whom he must yet render an account of his stewardship; in the meantime, he must perform his duty for the good of the commonwealth, *serving* the interests of those under him.

So too of the *economical power*, that of the husband, parent, master. There are not only duties pertaining to those relations, but mutual obligations wherein the power of the superior is to be subordinated to the interests of the inferior. The husband is the head of the wife and she is required to own him as her lord (1 Peter 3:6), but that gives him no right to act as a tyrant and make her the slave of his lusts. He is under bonds to love and cherish her, to give honour to her as unto the weaker vessel, to seek her happiness and do all in his power to lighten her burden.

Parents are to govern their children and not to tolerate insubordination, yet they must not provoke them to wrath by brutal treatment, but bring them up in the nurture and admonition of the Lord, teaching them to be truthful, industrious, honest, looking after the good of their souls as well as bodies.

Masters are bidden to give unto their servants 'that which is just and equal, knowing that *they* have a Master in heaven'

(Colossians 4:1) who will sanction no injustice and condone no harshness. God has so tied us one to another that everyone is to do his part in promoting the common good.

Power is bestowed upon men by God not for the purpose of their self-exaltation but for the benefit of those they rule. Power is to be exercised with goodwill and benevolence, and deference is to be rendered by the subordinate - not sullenly, but freely and gladly, as unto God. 'Brethren, ye have been called unto liberty: only use not liberty for an occasion to the flesh, but *by love serve* one another' (Galatians 5:13) interprets for us 'submitting yourselves one to another'. It is the *mutual* submission of brotherly love which is there enjoined, of that love which 'seeketh not her own', but ever labours for the good of its objects.

It is that mutual subjection which one Christian owes to another, not seeking to advance himself above his fellows and domineer over them, but which is selfless, bearing one another's burdens. It is in the exercise of *that* spirit we please God, adorn the gospel, and make it manifest that we are the followers of him who was meek and lowly in heart. It is by mortifying our pride and selfishness, by the exercise of mutual affection, by discharging the office of respect and kindness unto the children of God, we show forth that we have passed from death unto life.

'Be kindly affectioned one to another with brotherly love, in honour preferring one another' (Romans 12:10). The Greek word there for 'preferring' signifies to take the lead or set an example. Instead of waiting for others to honour or minister unto me, I should be beforehand in deferring unto them. Where Christian love be cultivated and exercised there is a thinking and acting respectfully unto our brethren and sisters. 'In lowliness of mind let each esteem other better than themselves' (Philippians 2:3).

That does not mean the father in Christ is to value the opinions of a spiritual babe more than his own, still less that he is to feign a respect for the spirituality of another which he does not honestly feel; but it does signify that if his heart be right, he will so discern the image of Christ in his people as to make deference in love to them both an easy and pleasant duty, putting their interests before his own; and judging himself faithfully, he will discover that 'the least of all saints' suits no man better than himself. The exercised and humble believer will rather put honour on his brethren than seek it for himself.

If then God has called you into the ministry, it is not that you may ape the peacock or set yourself up as a little pope. You are not called to lord it over God's vineyard but to *labour in it*, to minister unto his people. The greatest of the apostles declared, 'Though I be free from all, yet have I made myself *servant unto all*, that I might gain the more' (1 Corinthians 9:19). But one infinitely greater than Paul is your pattern. Behold him humbling himself to perform the most menial office, as he girded himself with a towel, stooped down and washed the feet of his disciples! And remember it is unto the ministers of his gospel that he said:

'If I then, your Lord and Master, have washed your feet; ye also ought to wash one another's feet. For I have given you an example, that ye should do as I have done to you. Verily, verily, I say unto you, The servant is not greater than his Lord; neither he that is sent greater than he that sent him' (John 13:14-16).

A haughty and arrogant spirit ill becomes *his* servants.

That holy balance between 'call no man your father upon the earth' and 'submitting yourselves one to another' was perfectly exemplified by the Lord Jesus, who though God incarnate was also Jehovah's Servant. If on the one hand we find that he refused to be in bondage to the doctrines and commandments of the Pharisees (Luke 11:38; Matthew 15:2), and overrode their traditions with his authoritative 'I say unto you' (Matthew 5:21, 22 etc.), on the other hand we behold him submitting unto every ordinance of God and perfectly exemplifying every aspect of lowly submission. As a child he was 'subject unto' his parents (Luke 2:51). Ere he began his ministry he submitted to be baptized of John, saying 'thus it becometh us to fulfil all righteousness' (Matthew 3:15). He sought not his own glory (John 8:50) but rather the glory of the one who sent him (John 7:18). He denied himself food and rest that he might minister to others (Mark 3:20). The whole of his time was spent in 'going about doing good' (Acts 10:38). He bore patiently and tenderly with the dullness of his disciples, and broke not the bruised reed nor quenched the smoking flax (Matthew 12:20). And he has left us an example that *we* should follow *his* steps.

Submitting ourselves one to another means according to each the right of private judgment and respecting his convictions. It imports a readiness to receive counsel and reproof from my brethren, as David did when he was king (Psalm 141:5). It connotes a cheerful denying of self as I seek their good. It signifies doing all in my power to minister unto their holiness and happiness. As one of the old worthies put it, 'The saints are trees of righteousness whose fruit is to be eaten by others; candles, which spend themselves in giving light and comfort to those about them'.

To obey this precept we require to be clothed with *humility*: it is the proud who cannot endure subjection, and who consider it beneath them to lend a helping hand to those less favoured. *Love* must be warm and active if superiors and inferiors are to treat one another with kindness and respect. Where love reigns none will be disdained or slighted. 'In the fear of God' this submission is to be rendered: in conscience to his command, with a regard for his glory.

CHAPTER 10

Grace Preparing for Glory

For the grace of God that bringeth salvation hath appeared to
all men, teaching us that, denying ungodliness and worldly
lusts, we should live soberly, righteously, and godly, in this
present world; looking for that blessed hope, and the glorious
appearing of the great God and our Saviour Jesus Christ
(Titus 2:11-13).

The opening 'For' looks back to verse 10. In the immediate
context the apostle had exhorted servants to walk amiably and
faithfully, so that they 'adorned the doctrine of God our
Saviour in all things'. It is deeply important that we should be
sound in doctrine, for error acts upon the soul the same as
poison does upon the body. Yes, it is very necessary that we
be sound in the Faith, for it is dishonouring to God and
injurious to ourselves to believe the Devil's lies, for that is
what false doctrine is. Then let us not despise *doctrinal*
preaching, for 'all Scripture is given by inspiration of God,
and is profitable for doctrine' (2 Timothy 3:16).

But there is something else which is equally important as
being sound in doctrine, namely, that we *adorn* it by our
conduct. The sounder I am in doctrine, the more loudly I
advertise my orthodox views, the more do I bring that doctrine
into reproach if my life be worldly and my walk carnal. How
earnestly we need to pray for Divine enablement that we may

'adorn the doctrine in all things'. We need the doctrine of Scripture written upon our hearts, moulding our character, regulating our ways, influencing our conduct. We 'adorn' the doctrine when we 'walk in newness of life', when we live each hour as those who must appear before the judgment seat of Christ. And we are to 'adorn the doctrine in *all* things': in every sphere we occupy, every relation we sustain, every circle God's providence brings us into.

The apostle now enforces what he had said in verse 10 by reminding us that 'the grace of God that bringeth salvation hath appeared to all men'. This is in blessed contrast from the law, which brings naught but 'condemnation'. But the grace of God bringeth *salvation*, and that in a twofold way: by what Christ has done *for* his people, and by what he works *in* them. 'He shall save his people from their sins' (Matthew 1:21): save from the guilt and penalty of sin, and from the love or power of sin. This grace of God 'hath appeared': it has broken forth like the light of the morning after a dark night. It has 'appeared' both objectively and subjectively - in the gospel and in our hearts: 'when it pleased God... to reveal his Son *in* me' (Galatians 1:16); 'God who commanded the light to shine out of darkness, hath shined *in our hearts*' (2 Corinthians 4:6).

The grace of God - his lovingkindness, his goodwill, his free favour - hath appeared 'to all men'. That expression is used in Scripture in two different senses: sometimes it means all *without exception*, as in 'all have sinned and come short of the glory of God'. In other passages it signifies all *without distinction*, as it does here - to the bondmen, as well as the free, to the servant as the master, to the Gentiles as to the Jews; to all kinds and conditions of men. But how may I know that the grace of God which bringeth salvation has appeared *to me*? A vitally important question is that, one which none who really values the eternal interests of his or her soul will treat lightly or take for granted. There are many who profess to be 'saved' but they give *no evidence* of it in their lives. Now here is the inspired answer.

'Teaching us that, denying ungodliness and worldly lusts.' Divine grace teaches its favoured recipients subjectively as well as objectively, effectually as well as theoretically. Grace in the heart prevents us from abusing grace in the head: it delivers us from making grace the lackey of sin. Where the grace of God brings salvation to the soul, it works effectually. And *what is it* that grace teaches? *Practical holiness*. Grace does not eradicate ungodliness and worldly lusts, but it causes us *to deny* them. And what but 'Divine grace' can? Philosophy cannot, or ethics, nor any form of human education or culture. But grace *does*, by the impulsive power of gratitude, by love's desire to please the Saviour, by instilling a determination to 'walk worthy of the vocation wherewith we are called'.

Alas, many who are glad to hear of the grace which brings salvation become restless when the preacher presses the truth that God's grace teaches to *deny*. That is a very unpalatable word in this age of self-pleasing and self-indulgence; but turn to Matthew 16:24, 'Then said Jesus unto his disciples, If any man will come after me, let him *deny* himself, and take up his cross, and follow me'. And again, 'Whosoever doth not bear his cross, and come after me, cannot be my disciple' (Luke 14:27): that is the unceasing demand of Christ, and naught but Divine grace working within can enable any one to meet it.

Grace teaches *negatively*: it teaches us to renounce evil. Dagon must first be cast down before the ark of God can be set up. The leaven must be excluded from our houses before the Lamb can be fed upon. The old man has to be put off if the new man is to be put on. Grace teaches a Christian to *mortify* his members which are upon the earth: 'to deny ungodliness and worldly lusts'. Grace teaches the believer to resist these evils, by preventing the flesh from *ruling* over him, and that, by refusing to allow sin to dominate his heart.

'Ungodliness' is failing to give *God* his due place in our hearts and lives. It is disregarding his precepts and commands. It is having preference for the creature, loving pleasure more than holiness; being unconcerned whether my conduct pleases or displeases the Lord. There are many forms of 'ungodliness' besides that of open infidelity and the grosser crimes of wickedness. We are guilty of 'ungodliness' when we are prayerless. We are guilty of 'ungodliness' when we look to and lean upon the creature; or when we fail to see God's hand in providence - ascribing our blessings to 'luck' or 'chance'. We are guilty of 'ungodliness' when we grumble at the weather.

'And worldly lusts': these are those affections and appetites which dominate and regulate the man of the world. It is the heart craving worldly objects, pleasures, honours, riches. It is an undue absorption with those things which serve only a temporary purpose and use. 'Worldly lusts' cause the things of heaven to be crowded out by the interests and concerns of earth. This may be done by things which are quite lawful in themselves, but through an immoderate use they gain possession of the heart. 'Worldly lusts' are 'the lusts of the flesh, and the lust of the eyes, and the pride of life' (1 John 2:16).

Now Divine grace is teaching the Christian to '*deny* ungodliness and worldly lusts'. It does this by putting upon him 'the fear of the Lord', so that he departs from evil. It does this by occupying the heart with a superior Object: when Christ was revealed to the heart of the Samaritan woman she '*left* her waterpot' (John 4:28). It does this by supplying the powerful motives and incentives to personal holiness. It does this by the indwelling Spirit resisting the flesh (Galatians 5:17). It does this by causing us to subordinate the interests of the body unto the higher interests of the soul.

Grace teaches *positively*. It is not sufficient that we 'deny ungodliness and worldly lusts', we must also '*live* soberly, righteously, and godly, in this present world'.

'Soberly' comes first because we cannot live righteously or godly without it: he who takes to himself more than is due or meet will not give men or God their portion. Unfortunately the word 'sober' is now generally restricted to the opposite of inebriation, but the Christian is to be sober in *all* things. Sobriety is the moderation of our affections in the pursuit and use of earthly things. We are to be temperate in eating, sleeping, recreation, dress. We need to be sober-minded, and not extremists. Only Divine grace can effectually teach sobriety, and if I am growing in grace, then I am becoming more sober. Grace does not remove natural inclinations and affections, but it *governs* them - it bridles their excess. The first thing, then, that grace teaches us positively is *self-control*. 'He that is slow to anger is better than the mighty; and he that *ruleth his spirit* than he that taketh a city' (Proverbs 16:32).

'Righteously.' This concerns our dealings with our fellows. It is giving to each his due, dealing honourably with all; injuring none, seeking the good of all. To live 'righteously' is doing unto others as we would have them do unto us; it is being truthful, courteous, considerate, kind, helpful. 'Do

good unto all men, especially unto those who are of the
household of faith', must be our constant aim. This is the
second half of the law's requirement, that we should 'love our
neighbour as ourselves'. Only Divine grace can effectually
'teach' us this. Naught but Divine Grace can counteract our
innate *selfishness*.

'Godly.' This is the attitude of our hearts towards God,
ever seeking his glory. Godliness is made up of three ingre-
dients, or more accurately, it issues from three springs: faith,
fear, love. Only by *faith* can we really apprehend God: 'Take
heed, brethren, lest there be in any of you an evil heart of
unbelief, in *departing from* the living God' (Hebrews 3:12).
Forty years ago we often heard the expression so and so is 'a
God-fearing man': the fact we rarely hear this now is a bad
sign. But there are two kinds of *fear*, a servile and a filial - a
dread of God and an awe of God. The first kind was seen in
Adam when he was afraid of the Lord and hid himself. The
second kind was exemplified by Joseph when tempted by the
wife of Potiphar: reverential fear restrained him. Only Divine
grace can 'teach' us this. While *love* constrains unto obedience: 'If ye love me, keep my commandments' (John 14:15).
It is only love's obedience which is acceptable unto God: the
heart melted by his goodness, now desiring to please him.

'Looking for that blessed hope, and the glorious appearing
of the great God and our Saviour Jesus Christ.' Now this must
not be divorced from its context, for there we are shown the
necessary prerequisite - *Grace preparing for Glory*. The
passage as a whole is made up of three parts: in the past, the
grace of God brought salvation to the believer; in the present,
Divine grace is teaching him, both negatively, and positively,
how to live acceptably unto God; third, in the future, the work

of Divine grace will be perfected in the believer, at the return of Christ.

Verse 13, then, is the necessary *sequel* to what has been before us in verses 11 and 12. My head may be filled with prophecy, I may be an ardent premillennarian, I may think and say that I am 'looking for that blessed Hope' *but*, unless Divine grace is teaching me to deny 'ungodliness and worldly lusts' and to 'live soberly, righteously, and godly, in this present world', then I am *deceiving myself*. Make no mistake upon that point. To be *truly* 'looking for that blessed hope' is a *spiritual* attitude: it is the longing of those whose hearts are right with God. Thus, our text may be summed up in three words: grace, godliness, glory.

Now our 'hope' is something more than a future *event*, concerning the details of which there may be room for considerable difference of opinion. Our hope is something more than the *next item* on God's prophetic programme. It is something more than a *place* in which we are going to spend eternity. The Christian's hope is a *person*. Have you noticed how prominently and emphatically that fact is presented in the Scriptures? 'I will come again, and receive you *unto myself*' (John 14:3); 'This *same Jesus* which is taken up from you into heaven shall so come in like manner' (Acts 1:11); 'We look *for the Saviour*' (Philippians 3:20); 'The coming *of the Lord* draweth nigh' (James 5:8) - not even the Great Tribulation draweth nigh, not the Millennium draweth nigh, nor even the Rapture draweth nigh, but the *coming of the Lord*. It is with his own blessed person that our poor hearts need to be occupied.

Here is a poor wife whose husband has been away for many months in distant lands, whose duty required him to go there.

News arrives that he is coming back home: the devoted wife is filled with joy at the prospect of the return of her husband. Is she puzzling her brains as to what will be his programme of action after he arrives? No, the all-absorbing thing for her is *himself* - her beloved is soon to appear before her.

Now do not misunderstand me: I am not saying that the plan of prophecy holds little of interest, or that it matters nothing to us what course Christ will follow; but that which I am seeking to emphasise is that the primary and grand point of the whole subject is having our prepared hearts fixed upon Christ himself. God would have us occupied not so much with prophetic details, as with the blessed person of his dear Son.

That 'blessed hope', then, which the Christian is 'looking for' is not an event, but a Person: Christ himself. 'And this is his name whereby he shall be called, THE LORD OUR RIGHTEOUS-NESS' (Jeremiah 23:6) - the Lord is our righteousness. 'For he is our peace' (Ephesians 2:13) - the Lord is our peace. 'When Christ, who is our life, shall appear' (Colossians 3:4) - the Lord is our life. 'By the commandment of God our Saviour, and Lord Jesus Christ, who is our hope' (1 Timothy 1:1) - the Lord is our hope.

To me 'that blessed hope' is summed up in three things. First, that Christ is coming to receive me *unto* himself. Second, that Christ will then make me *like* himself - for nothing less than *that* will satisfy him or the renewed heart. Third, that Christ is going to have me forever *with* himself - an eternity of bliss spent in his own immediate presence. Then will be answered his prayer ' Father, I will that they also, whom thou hast given me, be with me where I am; that they may behold my glory' (John 17:24).

Now '*looking for* that blessed Hope', for Christ himself, is *an attitude of heart*. The Christian 'looks' with the eyes of *faith*, and faith always rests alone upon God and his Word. Faith is not influenced by sensational items from the newspapers about the latest doings of Hitler and Mussolini etc. Scripture says, 'The coming of the Lord draweth nigh', and faith believes it. The Christian 'looks' with the eyes of *hope*, joyously anticipating perfect fellowship with its Beloved. The Christian 'looks' with the eyes of *love*, for nothing but his personal presence can satisfy him. It is an attitude of *anticipation:* Christ has given his sure promise that *he is coming*, but the exact *time* is withheld - that we may be in constant readiness. It is an attitude of *expectation*, for we do not 'look for' something we know will never happen. It is an attitude of *supplication*, the heart's response is, 'Even so, *come*, Lord Jesus.'

A final word upon Christ's title here: 'The glorious appearing of *the great God* and our Saviour Jesus Christ', or as Bagster's Interlinear more correctly renders it, 'And appearing of the glory, the great God and Saviour, of our Lord Jesus Christ'. Three things are suggested to us by Christ's being here called 'the great God'. First, it points a contrast from his first advent, when he appeared in humiliation and lowliness as the 'Servant'. Second, it shows us he is called 'God' not by way of courtesy, but by right of his Divine nature. Third, it evidences the fact that the Saviour is in no wise inferior to the Father, but his co-equal, 'the great God'.